Amsterdam
day BY day

1st Edition

by Haas Mroue

WILEY

Wiley Publishing, Inc.

Contents

Published by:

Wiley Publishing, Inc.

111 River St.
Hoboken, NJ 07030-5774

ISBN-13: 978-0-7645-9894-4
ISBN-10: 0-7645-9894-5

Editor: Christine Ryan
Production Editor: Heather Wilcox
Photo Editor: Richard Fox
Cartographer: Elizabeth Puhl
Production by Wiley Indianapolis Composition Services

For information on our other products and services or to obtain technical support, please contact our Customer Care Department within the U.S. at 800/762-2974, outside the U.S. at 317/572-3993 or fax 317/572-4002.

Wiley also publishes its books in a variety of electronic formats. Some content that appears in print may not be available in electronic formats.

Manufactured in China

5   4   3   2

A Note from the Publisher

Organizing your time. That's what this guide is all about.

Other guides give you long lists of things to see and do and then expect you to fit the pieces together. The Day by Day guides are different. These guides tell you the best of everything, and then they show you how to see it *in the smartest, most time-efficient way*. Our authors have designed detailed itineraries organized by time, neighborhood or special interest. And each tour comes with a bulleted map that takes you from stop to stop.

Hoping to admire some van Goghs, or buy some tulip bulbs to take back home? Planning to pedal along some canals, or take a whirl-wind tour of the very best that Amsterdam has to offer? Whatever your interest or schedule, the Day by Days give you the smartest route to follow. Not only do we take you to the top sights and attractions, but we introduce you to those special moments that only locals know about—those "finds" that turn tourists into travelers.

The Day by Days are also your top choice if you're looking for one complete guide for all your travel needs. The best hotels and restaurants for every budget, the greatest shopping values, the wildest nightlife—it's all here.

Why should you trust our judgment? Because our authors personally visit each place they write about. They're an independent lot who say what they think and would never include places they wouldn't recommend to their best friends. They're also open to suggestions from readers. If you'd like to contact them, please send your comments my way at mspring@wiley.com, and I'll pass them on.

Enjoy your Day by Day guide—the most helpful travel companion you can buy. And have the trip of a lifetime.

Warm regards,

Michael Spring,
Publisher
Frommer's Travel Guides

About the Author

Haas Mroue is a freelance travel writer based in the United States; he graduated from UCLA Film School and holds an M.A. in Literature from the University of Colorado, Boulder. He has been published in many journals and magazines, including *The Literary Review, Virtuoso Life Magazine, Out & About,* and the *Michigan Quarterly Review.* He has written for Encyclopaedia Britanica, *National Geographic,* and Berlitz Travel Guides, and his creative work has aired on the BBC World Service and on Starz! cable channel. He's the author of *Frommer's Memorable Walks in Paris, Frommer's Paris from $95 a Day,* and is a contributor to *Frommer's Europe from $85 a Day, Frommer's South America,* and *Frommer's Argentina & Chile.*

Acknowledgments

Haas Mroue would like to thank Nathalie Van Wees, Kess Connelly, Catherine Leitner, and the very hospitable Mrs. Fontijn. Thanks to all for making my stay in Amsterdam so memorable. This book is dedicated to Mary Beth and Hubert Morsink—for friendships that last more than just one lifetime.

An Additional Note

Please be advised that travel information is subject to change at any time—and this is especially true of prices. We therefore suggest that you write or call ahead for confirmation when making your travel plans. The authors, editors, and publisher cannot be held responsible for the experiences of readers while traveling. Your safety is important to us, however, so we encourage you to stay alert and be aware of your surroundings.

Star Ratings, Icons & Abbreviations

Every hotel, restaurant, and attraction listing in this guide has been ranked for quality, value, service, amenities, and special features using a **star-rating system.** Hotels, restaurants, attractions, shopping, and nightlife are rated on a scale of zero stars (recommended) to three stars (exceptional). In addition to the star-rating system, we also use a **kids icon** to point out the best bets for families.

The following **abbreviations** are used for credit cards:

AE	American Express	DISC	Discover	V	Visa
DC	Diners Club	MC	MasterCard		

Frommers.com

Now that you have the guidebook to a great trip, visit our website at **www.frommers.com** for travel information on more than 3,000 destinations. With features updated regularly, we give you instant access to the most current trip-planning information available. At Frommers.com, you'll also find the best prices on airfares, accommodations, and car rentals—and you can even book travel online through our travel booking partners.

A Note on Prices

Frommer's provides exact prices in each destination's local currency. As this book went to press, the rate of exchange was 1€ = US$1.30. Rates of exchange are constantly in flux; for up-to-the-minute information, consult a currency-conversion website such as www.oanda.com/convert/classic.

In the Take a Break and Best Bets section of this book, we have used a system of dollar signs to show a range of costs for one night in a hotel (the price of a double-occupancy room) or the cost of an entrée at a restaurant. Use the following table to decipher the dollar signs:

Cost	Hotels	Restaurants
$	under $100	under $10
$$	$100–$200	$10–$20
$$$	$200–$300	$20–$30
$$$$	$300–$400	$30–$40
$$$$$	over $400	over $40

An Invitation to the Reader

In researching this book, we discovered many wonderful places—hotels, restaurants, shops, and more. We're sure you'll find others. Please tell us about them, so we can share the information with your fellow travelers in upcoming editions. If you were disappointed with a recommendation, we'd love to know that, too. Please write to:

Frommer's Amsterdam Day by Day, 1st Edition
Wiley Publishing, Inc. • 111 River St. • Hoboken, NJ 07030-5774

13 Favorite
Moments

13 Favorite **Moments**

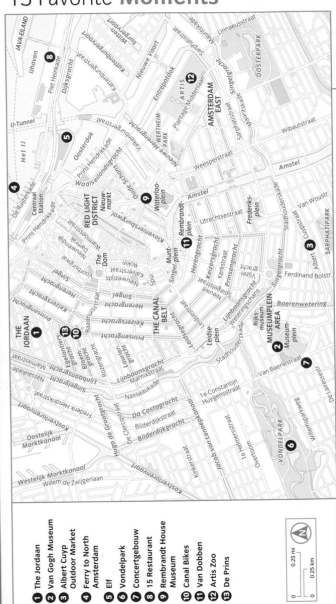

1 The Jordaan
2 Van Gogh Museum
3 Albert Cuyp Outdoor Market
4 Ferry to North Amsterdam
5 Elf
6 Vondelpark
7 Concertgebouw
8 15 Restaurant
9 Rembrandt House Museum
10 Canal Bikes
11 Van Dobben
12 Artis Zoo
13 De Prins

0   0.25 mi
0   0.25 km

So many of my favorite moments in Amsterdam are outdoors. Even in midwinter this city bustles with an infectious energy on its narrow streets, lovely canals, and charming bridges. Whichever time you choose to visit, you'll be struck, I'm sure, by how lively and bright this city really is. Here are some of my favorite moments, both outdoors and indoors, that have placed Amsterdam so close to my heart.

❶ Strolling in the Jordaan. The first thing I do after arriving in Amsterdam—whether I'm here in the dead of winter or the brilliance of summer—is to take a long stroll in the Jordaan up and down its beautiful canals. I like to look at the buildings and the houseboats and then stop for a strong coffee served with syrupy condensed milk at a neighborhood cafe. Then I'm ready for my first day in this colorful and architecturally rich city. *See p 52.*

❷ Admiring the paintings at the van Gogh Museum, late in the afternoon just before the museum closes, is one of the highlights to a trip to Amsterdam. That's when the usually crowded second-floor gallery is almost empty and I can stand there, lost in my own world, admiring Vincent's brush strokes

You can see Sunflowers *and many other famous works at the van Gogh Museum.*

without being shoved around by the throngs. *See p 7.*

❸ Picking out fruit at the Albert Cuyp Outdoor Market, early in the morning (between 8–9am) as the stands are being prepared for a long day of shoppers, is a quintessential Amsterdam moment. I like to watch the fresh fish being laid out on ice, imagining how, not long ago, it was swimming in the North Sea. *See p 17.*

❹ Catching the ferry to North Amsterdam, from behind Centraal Station, immediately gives me a sense of space. The river is full of boats, ferries, and barges, and I ride the free ferry to the other bank and back, just to take in the views. *See p 41.*

A flower stand at the Albert Cuyp market.

5 **Cocktails at Elf,** with its sweeping views of the city, are a requisite for any first-time visitor to Amsterdam. The large, expansive, 11th-floor restaurant and bar boasts floor-to-ceiling windows, great drinks, and tasty appetizer platters. *See p 25.*

6 **Strolling in Vondelpark** on a sunny afternoon makes me feel as if I'm a million miles from any city. The English-style manicured gardens are lovely, and when I'm lucky, I can stop and smell the roses, which bloom in late summer. *See p 78.*

7 **An evening at the Concertgebouw,** an acoustically perfect concert hall that many top conductors visit, is one of my favorite ways to spend a night in Amsterdam. *See p 116.*

8 **Watching the hectic choreography** of the gorgeous waitstaff as they serve their trendy clientele at Jamie Oliver's 15 is mesmerizing. If you fail to make reservations, just sit at the bar and order appetizers (it's cheaper, anyway) as you take in the heady atmosphere of the young chefs in action in the open kitchen. *See p 96.*

9 **Standing alone in Rembrandt's bedroom** over 500 years after he last slept there fills me with awe. This is where he refreshed himself after a long day at the canvas, I think to

You can get a whole new perspective on Amsterdam from a canal bike.

myself over and over again. Come early in the day or right at closing time and you'll have a good chance at being alone too. *See p 19.*

10 **Peeking at houseboats** at eye-level as I pedal a canal bike lets me see Amsterdam from a different angle. The Jordaan canals are especially dense with lived-in houseboats. *See p 82.*

11 **Eating a raw-herring sandwich** with pickles and onions with the locals at Van Dobben is what I do on my first day in Amsterdam. Somehow, the taste of the North Sea helps whet my appetite for all that's to come. *See p 100.*

12 **A morning at the zoo** makes me feel like a kid again. I walk to centrally located Artis Zoo to watch the animals being fed—a minisafari in the middle of this big city. *See p 34.*

13 **A frothy Heineken at a brown cafe** at dusk is my favorite ending to any day in Amsterdam. I like to sit outside, canalside at De Prins on Prinsengracht, and stretch my legs, watching the houseboats bobbing up and down in the water. *See p 9.* ●

Vondelpark is the perfect place to relax on a sunny day.

The Best **in One Day**

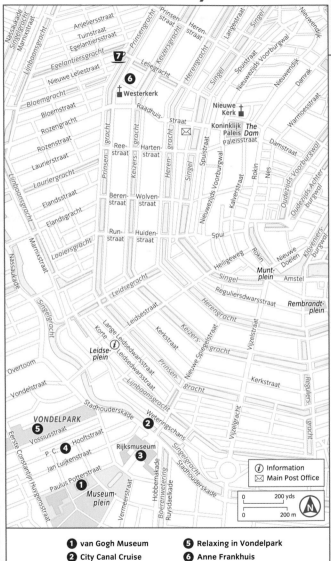

1. van Gogh Museum
2. City Canal Cruise
3. Rijksmuseum
4. Window-Shopping on P.C. Hoofstraat
5. Relaxing in Vondelpark
6. Anne Frankhuis
7. De Prins

Amsterdam is a very compact city, so this 1-day tour allows you to see the major highlights with minimal time spent on public transportation. Wear comfortable shoes and be sure to look both ways as you cross major intersections—bicyclists follow no rules here and they travel at alarming speeds. START: **Tram 2 or 5 to Museumplein.**

❶ ★★★ van Gogh Museum.
This gem of a museum houses the world's largest collection of van Gogh's work: 200 paintings, 580 drawings, and over 700 letters by Vincent himself (most written to his brother, Theo). A four-story building designed by Gerrit Rietveld houses the permanent collection. Although most of the work here is by van Gogh, the third floor includes an impressive number of paintings by Impressionist artists such as Monet, Seurat, Pissarro, Gauguin, and Toulouse-Lautrec. An adjacent building in the shape of an ellipse, designed by Kisho Kurokawa and built in 1999, houses the temporary exhibits. These exhibits, which change every 3 or 4 months, often include some of van Gogh's drawings. Check the museum website for the schedule. ⏲ *3 hr.*

Arrive at 9:45am to beat the crowds; buy tickets from the museum's website to cut down on wait time. Paulus Potterstraat 7 (at Museumplein). ☎ *020/570-5200. www.vangogh museum.nl. Admission 13€. Sat–Thurs 10am–6pm; Fri 10am–10pm. Closed Jan 1. Tram: 2 or 5 to Museumplein.*

❷ ★★ City Canal Cruise.
There's no better way to discover Amsterdam than from its canals. Sure, it's touristy, but I can't think of a better way to see a large chunk of Amsterdam in a short time. You can opt to sit outside if the weather permits or settle into a comfortable seat indoors. The boat loops northward on the western canals, circles Centraal Station, and loops back to the departure point along the eastern canals. There's commentary in

A man studies one of van Gogh's self portraits.

Touring Amsterdam by canal boat can help you get a feel for the city.

English, so you'll know what you're seeing. ⏱ 1½ hr. *Stadhouderskade.* ☎ *020/679-1370. www.canal-cruises. nl. Departures every 30 min. 10am– 6pm Apr–Sept; every hour 10am– 6pm Oct–Mar. Adults 9€; children 5.50€. Tram: 2 or 5 to Hobbema- straat, behind the Rijksmuseum.*

❸ ★★★ **Rijksmuseum.** Petrus Cuypers (1827–1921), the "grandfa- ther of modern Dutch architecture," designed this museum in a monu- mental Dutch neo-Renaissance style. Cuypers, a Catholic, slipped in more than a dab of neo-Gothic, too, causing the country's thoroughly Protestant King William III to scorn what he called "that cathedral." The building opened in 1885 to a less- than-enthusiastic public reception. Most of the museum is closed for major renovations until the summer of 2008, but a small section of the museum, The Philips Wing, will remain open throughout the renova- tion. Rembrandt and Vermeer lovers, don't panic: You can still see *Nightwatch* and *The Kitchen Maid*. In fact, you'll find an entire room filled with Rembrandts. Three other galleries are dedicated to Vermeer, Frans Hals, and Jan Steen. ⏱ 1½ hr. *Jan Luijkenstraat 1.* ☎ *020/674- 7000. www.rijksmuseum.nl. Daily 9am–6pm. Closed Jan. 1. Admission 9€. Tram: 2 or 5 to Hobbemastraat.*

van Gogh: 10 Years of Genius

The second floor of the van Gogh Museum's permanent exhibit gives you a fascinating chronological insight into van Gogh's life and work. Although his career as a painter lasted only 10 years—during which time he completed over 900 paintings—you'll see stunning shifts in style and color as you move from one year and one geo- graphical area to another. For example, compare the dark and somber *Potato Eaters* from his earliest work in Holland in 1885 to the light and airy *View of the Roofs of Paris*, completed just a year later.

The paintings van Gogh completed in Arles—like his famous *Bedroom at Arles* (1888)—explode with color. There are several lesser-known paintings from the last year of his life, including the somewhat ominous *Wheatfield Under Thundercloud*, painted shortly before his suicide in 1890.

④ ★★★ Window-Shopping on P.C. Hoofstraat. The city's most upscale shopping district lies just a block from the Rijksmuseum, so those with shopping aspirations should take advantage of the opportunity to spend an hour strolling the short but oh-so-chic P.C. Hoofstraat. You'll find the quintessential jet-set boutiques such as Louis Vuitton, Armani, Dolce & Gabbana, Ralph Lauren, and Gucci clustered on this primo stretch of real estate. ⏲ *30–60 min. Shops open Mon–Sat 10am–6pm. Tram: 2 or 5 to Hobbemastraat.*

⑤ ★★★ Relaxing in Vondelpark. A 2-minute stroll from the Rijksmuseum and P.C. Hoofstraat brings you to the largest and most beautiful park in Amsterdam. Vondelpark is 44 hectares (110 acres) of peace and quiet, a cherished open space in this terribly dense city. Lovely benches overlook small ponds, walking trails, and bike trails. See also the tour of Vondelpark on p 78. ⏲ *30 min. Enter through the gates on the corner of Vossiusstraat and Stadhouderskade. Open 24 hr. Tram: 2 or 5 to Hobbemastraat.*

⑥ ★★★ Anne Frankhuis. It's about a 30-minute walk from Vondelpark to the Anne Frankhuis (or you can catch a tram). It was in this typical Amsterdam canal house that 13-year-old Anne Frank kept her famous diary. For 2 years during World War II, the Frank family hid in near-total silence in these rooms, before Nazi forces raided the house and deported the family to concentration camps. You can see where young Anne pinned up photos of her favorite actress, Deanna Durbin, and view an original copy of Anne's diary. Protective Plexiglas panels have been placed over some walls, but little else has changed since the Franks lived here. Almost a million visitors a year tour this house; be prepared to spend some time waiting to enter.

⏲ *1½ hr. Arrive after 4pm to avoid long lines, especially in summer. Prinsengracht 263 (at Westermarkt).* ☎ *020/556-7105. www.unnefrank.nl. Apr–Aug daily 9am–9pm; Sept–Mar daily 9am–7pm; Jan 1 & Dec 25 noon–7pm; May 4 9am–7pm; Dec 16 & 31 9am–5pm. Closed Yom Kippur. Admission 7.50€. Tram: 6, 13, 14, or 17 to Westermarkt.*

⑦ ★★ De Prins. After a long day of sightseeing, relax with the locals at a traditional "brown cafe" (so named for the old, smoke-stained walls). One of my favorites is just across from the Anne Frankhuis. Choose from a great selection of Dutch and Belgian beers and coffees, and try a traditional snack like *bitterballen* (fried minced-meat-and-potato balls) or chunks of Gouda cheese dipped in hot mustard. *Prinsengracht 124.* ☎ *020/624-9382. $.*

The attic where Anne Frank and her family lived for 2 years.

The Best **in Two Days**

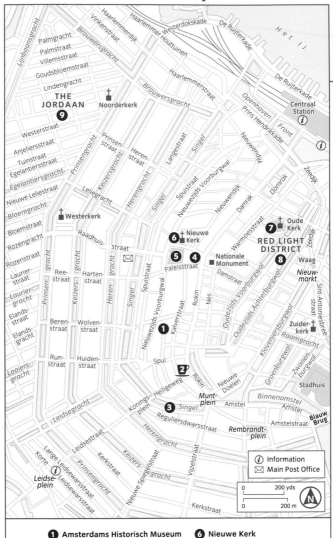

1. Amsterdams Historisch Museum
2. Kalvertoren Café & Brasserie
3. Flower Market
4. The Dam
5. Koninklijk Paleis
6. Nieuwe Kerk
7. Oude Kerk
8. Red Light District
9. The Jordaan

If you followed the "Best in One Day" tour, then you've already visited the city's most popular attractions and gotten an overview of the city from a canal cruise. Today you'll dig further into Amsterdam's history and architecture by visiting some of its monuments, smaller museums, and neighborhoods. You'll also stroll around the flower market and take a peek at the infamous Red Light District.
START: **Tram: 1, 2, 4, 5, 9, 14, 16, 24, or 25 to Spui.**

❶ ★★★ Amsterdams Historisch Museum (Amsterdam Historical Museum). Starting your day at this fascinating historical museum will give you a much deeper understanding of everything you'll see as you tour the rest of the city. The museum is housed in a former orphanage dating back to the 17th century (a small part of it dates back to 1578, when it was a convent). Gallery by gallery, century by century, you learn how a small fishing village founded around 1200 became a major sea power and trading center. Many exhibits focus on the 17th-century golden age, when Amsterdam was the richest city in the world. Art lovers will enjoy seeing famous paintings by Dutch masters explained in the context of their time and place in history. A beautiful scale model from 1677 shows what is now the Royal Palace (stop ❺ on this tour); some of its outer walls and the roof have been removed to give you a bird's-eye look inside. Lots of hands-on exhibits and some interesting video displays round out the experience.
🕐 *2 hr. Kalverstraat 92, Nieuwezijds Voorburgwal 357 & Sint-Luciensteeg 27.* ☎ *020/523-1822. www.ahm.nl. Admission 6€. Mon–Fri 10am–5pm; Sat–Sun & holidays 11am–5pm. Closed Jan 1, Apr 30, Dec 25. Tram: 1, 2, 4, 5, 9, 14, 16, 24, or 25 to Spui.*

An exhibit hall in the Amsterdam Historical Museum.

❷ ★★ Kalvertoren Café & Brasserie. I love to stop at the Kalvertoren in the late morning before the lunch rush and take in the heavenly 360-degree views of Amsterdam. If the weather is fine, you can grab a seat on the top-floor terrace, but the views from the floor-to-ceiling windows in the expansive lower dining room are equally panoramic. My favorite snack is a slathering of goat cheese on toasted focaccia with fresh tomatoes. The salade niçoise is excellent, too, and fried eggs with ham and cheese make a perfect late breakfast. *Top floor of the Kalvertoren shopping mall, enter on Singel 457 & take the elevator to the 3rd floor.* ☎ *020/427-3901. Daily 11am–10pm. $$.*

Gardeners will enjoy choosing from the large variety of tulip bulbs at Amsterdam's Flower Market.

❸ ★★ **Flower Market.** Since you're in the heart of Amsterdam's main shopping street, Kalverstraat, you may want to spend some time browsing. When you've had your fill, head two streets south to Singel (close to Muntplein) where you'll find the Bloemenmarkt (Flower Market). The market floats on a row of permanently moored barges, exploding with color and hundreds of flowers. Fresh tulips here cost about the same as those sold at the flower stands around town, so I don't recommend buying flowers and carrying them around all day. But it's a good place to pick up ready-to-travel packets of tulip bulbs that slip easily into your backpack or purse. *On Singel at Muntplein. Daily 8am– 8pm. Tram: 4, 9, 14, 16, 24, or 25.*

❹ **The Dam.** The Dam square is the epicenter of Amsterdam. It's the site of the original dam built across the Amstel River in the 13th century, hence the name. It's not particularly grand—the surrounding buildings are a mix of architectural styles, and pedestrians, bikes, trams, and cars perpetually jam the surrounding streets. But several of the city's important monuments can be found here: **The Royal Palace, The National Monument,** and the **New Church.** Take a walk (beware of those trams!) around the National Monument, a white column erected in 1956 as a tribute to Dutch citizens who died during the Nazi occupation during World War II. Urns filled with soil from the various states of the Netherlands and its former possessions overseas sit behind the monument (which was sculpted by Dutch artist John Radecker). ⏱ *15 min. Tram: 1, 2, 4, 5, 6, 9, 13, 14, 16, 17, 24, or 25 to the Dam.*

The Dam.

Old Church.

5 ★★ **Koninklijk Paleis (Royal Palace).** This is still the official home of the reigning king or queen of the Netherlands, though Queen Beatrix prefers to live in The Hague. The palace (1648–55), originally designed as a Town Hall, has a solid, neoclassical facade. The building didn't become a palace until 1808. The interior is filled with early-19th-century furniture, chandeliers, and marble floors. The most interesting room is the high-ceilinged Burgerzaal (Citizens Chamber), where the maps inlaid on the marble floors show Amsterdam as the center of the world. The palace is closed to visitors during periods of royal residence and state receptions. Call ahead for information. ⏲ *1 hr. Dam Sq.* ☎ *020/620-4060. www.koninklijkhuis.nl. Admission 4.50€. Easter holidays & June–Aug daily 11am–5pm; Sept to mid-Dec & mid-Feb to May (except Easter holidays), generally Tues–Thurs 12:30–5pm (open days & hours vary; check before going).*

6 ★ **Nieuwe Kerk (New Church).** Originally built in the 14th century as the city's second Catholic church, much of New Church was destroyed by fire in the 17th century (look for the carved gilded ceiling above the choir, which survived the fire). But a great deal of its original neo-Gothic grandeur has since been restored, and all the Dutch monarchs are inaugurated here. Don't miss the elaborately carved altar and the great pipe organ (from about 1645), which is still used for concerts. In the south transept, the lower-right corner of the stained-glass windows depicts Queen Wilhelmina surrounded by courtiers at her inauguration ⏲ *30 min. The*

One of New Church's elaborate stained-glass windows.

The Royal Household

Although the queen's official residence is the Royal Palace, she does not own it, nor does she own any of her other residences. The state makes them available to her and allocates a budget of about 4,000,000€ per year to manage her royal household. Her salary is separate. She earns a net income of 746,000€; the amount is not taxable. She pays taxes only on her private assets.

Dam (next to the Royal Palace). 020/638-6909. www.nieuwekerk. nl. *Admission varies with different events; free when there's no special exhibit. Daily 10am–6pm.*

7 ★★ Oude Kerk (Old Church). Just a few minutes' walk from New Church, you'll find the late-Gothic, triple-nave Old Church, which was begun in 1250 and completed with the extension of the bell tower in 1566. Rembrandt's wife lies in vault 28K, which bears the simple inscription "Saskia Juni 1642." The magnificent 1728 open organ is regularly used for recitals. You can climb the church tower on an hourly guided tour (given in English) for a great view of Old Amsterdam and the

Old Church's famous organ.

adjacent Red Light District. ⏱ *30 min. Oudekerksplein (at Oudezijds Voorburgwal).* 020/625-8284. www. oudekerk.nl. *Admission 4€. Church Mon–Sat 11am–5pm; Sun 1–5pm. Tower June–Sept Wed–Sun 2–4pm; Sept–Apr Sun–Fri 1–5pm, Sat 11–5pm. Closed Jan 1, Apr 30.*

8 Red Light District. Amsterdam's Red Light District is one of its best-known "attractions," with red lights illuminating minimally clad prostitutes on display behind glass windows along medieval alleyways. There are also live, hard-core sex shows that leave nothing to the imagination. Some of you may be repulsed by the sight of flesh for sale; for some it's just a fascinating window into the world's oldest profession. The Old Church is on the fringes of the Red Light District, so you can simply cross the canal and stroll up and down Oudezijds Achterburgwal. The very narrow alleyways leading away from the canal are also lined with glass "cages." It's not unsafe to meander here, especially before dark. You can skip it and head northwest from the Old Church to Warmoestraat, a pedestrian-only street lined with bars, funky sex shops, and "coffee shops" where patrons are as likely to order marijuana as they are coffee. From Oudezijds Achterburgwal, head back toward the Old Church, cross Oudezijds Voorburgwal and you'll hit Warmoestraat. Continue

A woman in the Red Light District waits for a customer.

along Warmoestraat and you'll find yourself facing Centraal Station.

🕐 *15–30 min. Dusk is the best time to visit the Red Light District, though it's open 24 hr.*

❾ ★★★ **Relaxing in the Jordaan.** It feels miles away from the crowded, sometimes seedy center where you've spent most of the day, yet the Jordaan is almost adjacent to Centraal Station and the best place to relax after a day of sightseeing. It's the most hip and unpretentiously elegant neighborhood in all of Amsterdam, its lovely canals lined with houseboats and its streets full of quaint boutiques and delightful cafes. If you have the time and energy, check out the walking tour of the Jordaan on p 52. Also consider staying for dinner (see the restaurant reviews in chapter 6).

A Behind-the-Scenes Look at the Dutch Sex Industry

The Red Light District in Amsterdam dates back to the 13th century, when the city emerged as Europe's leading port and sailors returned from long trips desperate for female companionship. By 1850, with a little over 200,000 residents in the city, there were already over 200 brothels. Now, the sex industry is a $1-billion business in the Netherlands, roughly 5% of the Dutch economy. But to this day, there's debate within the government as to how to regulate this industry. Some of the more mundane rules change constantly (such as: Can a prostitute claim lingerie on her income tax as a business write-off?), but the health department is very strict with its regulations. There are rules on everything from how hot the water needs to be before a prostitute washes her underwear to how long the women's nails can be. Recent statistics claim that over 60% of the women working in the sex industry are foreign, the majority of them new migrants from eastern Europe and Asia. The women come from all walks of life and for some this is just a second job to earn extra cash. Some are young students, some are housewives. In many instances neither their parents nor their husbands know of their second job. Women that you see in windows in the Red Light District can expect to earn 60€ to 150€ per customer, depending on what is asked of them. High-class prostitutes (found through an upmarket escort service or luxury brothel) can pull in over 1,000€ a night.

The Best **in Three Days**

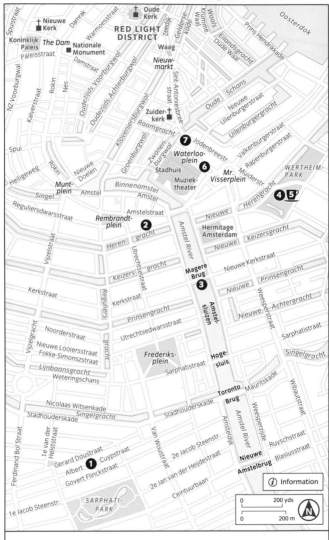

- **1** Albert Cuyp Outdoor Market
- **2** Museum Willet-Holthuysen
- **3** Magere Brug
- **4** Hortus Botanicus
- **5** Orangery Café
- **6** Waterlooplein Flea Market
- **7** Museum Het Rembrandt House

If you've followed the "Best in One" and "Best in Two Day" tours, then you've already seen many of the city's highlights. It's time to slow down a bit, blend in with the locals, meander around the markets, and take in some smaller museums. On this tour you'll also get a chance to (literally) stop and smell the roses at the relaxing Botanical Garden. START: **Tram 16, 24, or 25 to Albert Cuypstraat.**

The carefully restored kitchen at Museum Willet-Holthuysen.

❶ ★★ Albert Cuyp Outdoor Market. I love coming to the Albert Cuyp Market in the morning, getting lost in the frenzy of shoppers, and marveling at the rows of fresh fish, fruit, vegetables, and textiles on display. The market lies in the heart of The Pijp, a residential neighborhood full of young professionals. The area is slightly more affordable than the Jordaan and therefore attracts a somewhat younger crowd. Along the streets that intersect Albert Cuyp, you'll find many cafes where you can get a quick pick-me-up of strong coffee or tea. ⏱ *1 hr. Albert Cuypstraat,*

between Van der Helstraat und Sweelinckstraat. Mon–Sat 9am–6pm. Tram 16, 24, or 25 to Albert Cuypstraat.

❷ ★★ Museum Willet-Holthuysen. This is one of the best-preserved 17th-century canal houses in Amsterdam. It was built in 1687 and renovated several times before its last owner, Mrs. Willet-Holthuysen, willed the mansion and her fine-art collection to the city in 1885. Among the most interesting rooms are a Victorian-era bedroom on the second floor, a large reception room with tapestry wall panels,

Fun Facts & Figures

In Amsterdam you'll find one million permanent residents, more than a million visitors each month, 600,000 flower bulbs in its parks and public gardens, 1,281 bridges (8 of them wooden drawbridges), 400,000 bicycles, 220,000 trees, 260 city trams, 6,800 16th-, 17th-, and 18th-century buildings, 1,400 cafes and bars, 755 restaurants, 206 paintings by van Gogh, and 22 paintings by Rembrandt.

Skinny Bridge at night.

and an 18th-century basement kitchen set up to look as though the cook has just stepped out to go shopping. Be sure to peek out at the impressively restored 18th-century formal garden. ⏱ *45 min. Herengracht 605 (near the Amstel River).* ☎ *020/523-1822. www.willet holthuysen.nl. Admission 4€. Mon–Fri 10am–5pm; Sat–Sun 11am–5pm. Closed Jan 1, Apr 30, Dec 25. Tram: 4, 9, or 14 to Rembrandtplein.*

❸ ★★★ **Magere Brug (Skinny Bridge).** After leaving the museum, head west toward the Amstel, then south along the riverbank for a quick 15-minute detour to see this fantastic bridge. Legend has it that the Magere Brug was built to make it easier for two sisters (of the Mager family) who lived on opposite sides of the river to visit each other. The double-drawbridge was built in 1672 of African azobe wood; it was renovated in 1969. Come during the day to see the unusual wood details, or at night to see it twinkling with hundreds of lights. If you're lucky, you might see the bridge master raising it to allow boats through. ⏱ *15 min. The bridge spans the Amstel between Kerkstraat and Nieuwe Kerkstraat.*

❹ ★★ kids **Hortus Botanicus (Botanical Garden).** Retrace your steps north to this oasis of green, a treasure trove of tropical plants taken from the former Dutch colonies of Indonesia, Surinam, and the Antilles. Established in 1682, this lovely garden explodes with the colors and scents of over 250,000 flowers and 115,000 plants and trees. The city's physicians and apothecaries originally created it as a garden for medicinal herbs. The first coffee plant in Europe was brought here in 1706 by a Dutch merchant who smuggled it out of Ethiopia. The three-climate greenhouse gets progressively warmer as you walk through it—most

The butterfly house at the Botanical Garden is a big hit with kids.

Waterlooplein Flea Market.

of the plants here come from Australia and South Africa. There's also an herb garden, a desert greenhouse, and a butterfly house with free-flying giant butterflies that kids will love. ⏱ *1 hr. Plantage Middenlaan 2A.* ☎ *020/625-9021. www. dehortus.nl. Admission 6€. Feb–Nov Mon–Fri 9am–5pm, Sat–Sun 10am–5pm; Dec–Jan Mon–Fri 9am–4pm, Sat–Sun 10am–4pm. Closed Jan 1 & Dec 25. Tram: 9 or 14 to Plantage Middenlaan.*

5 ★★★ **Orangery Café.** This cafe, in the Botanical Garden, is one of my absolute favorite places to unwind and recharge. It's housed in the beautiful 1875 Orangery building, designed to shelter orange trees in winter. The cafe serves one of the best apple pies in the city, along with delicious salads and imaginative sandwiches. If you score one of the outdoor tables, you can listen to the birds chirping as you eat. *Inside the Hortus Botanicus, Plantage Middenlaan 2A. Open daily 11am–4pm. $$.*

6 ★ **Waterlooplein Flea Market.** Another 10-minute walk brings you to this quintessential classic Amsterdam flea market. In its glory, before World War II, you could find amazing antiques and even paintings by the masters at bargain prices. Today you can meander from one merchant's tent to another, hunting for good deals on anything from cooking pots to used CDs, leather jackets, watches, and colorful sweaters. I come here just to people-watch. It's also a good place to try some street food, like french fries eaten Dutch-style—with mayonnaise. ⏱ *30 min. Mon–Sat 10am–5pm. Waterlooplein. Tram: 9 or 14 to Waterlooplein.*

7 ★★★ **Museum Het Rembrandt House (Rembrandt House Museum).** Just a few minutes' walk from Waterlooplein lies the beautifully preserved house where Rembrandt van Rijn lived and worked in the 17th century. He bought the three-story house in 1639 when he was Amsterdam's most fashionable portrait painter. In this house, Rembrandt's son Titus was born and his wife Saskia died (you may have seen her tomb at the Old Church yesterday). Due to his extravagant lifestyle, Rembrandt was bankrupt when he left the house in 1658, and it wasn't until 1906 that the building was restored as a museum. Today the old house looks the way it did when Rembrandt lived and worked here—the 17th-century furnishings closely match the detailed descriptions

Rembrandt gave of his possessions in his 1656 bankruptcy petition. You'll see the kitchen and maid's bedroom on the ground floor, and upstairs you'll find Rembrandt's bedroom, living room, and the studio, where he painted such works as his infamous *Nightwatch*. You can also see his printing press and some 250 of his etchings and drawings, which hang on the walls. ⏲ *1 hr. Arrive here an hour or two before closing to avoid the crowds. Visit on Wed or weekends if you're interested in etching demonstrations. Jodenbreestraat 4–6 (at Waterlooplein).* ☎ *020/520-0400. www.rembrandthuis.nl. Admission 7€. Mon–Sat 10am-5pm; Sun & holidays 1–5pm. Closed Jan. 1. Tram: 9 or 14 to Waterlooplein.* ●

Rembrandt House Museum.

Below Sea Level

Amsterdammers have always had an intimate relationship with the sea. All those centuries of listening to the waves beating against the dikes raised against its clear and present danger—how could it be otherwise? But that its solid, timeless buildings stand, and its 740,000 inhabitants live, where waves should by all rights be lapping, is a difficult concept for foreigners to grasp.

Amsterdam lies up to 5.5m (18 ft.) below mean sea level. That it does not lie beneath the sea is due to stringent protective measures and Dutch engineering skill, which together have kept the city's collective head above water for most of the past 800 years.

If the coast defenses that protect Amsterdam should ever be overwhelmed, most of the city would vanish beneath the waves (did you check that insurance policy?). A graphic cross-section of the topography between the North Sea and Amsterdam, which you can buy printed on postcards and posters, shows that Vondelpark would become a lake, the Metro system would be well and truly drowned, and the trams would float away, but if you happened to be standing on top of the Oude Kerk tower you wouldn't even get your feet wet.

Amsterdam for **Art Lovers**

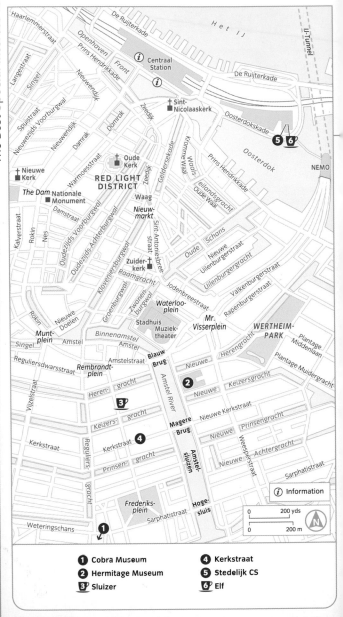

1 Cobra Museum

2 Hermitage Museum

3 Sluizer

4 Kerkstraat

5 Stedelijk CS

6 Elf

Amsterdam is a feast for art lovers. With 22 Rembrandts, 206 van Goghs, numerous Vermeers, and a plethora of Impressionist and post-Impressionist paintings scattered throughout the city, art lovers will be in heaven here. This tour is for art lovers who would have already made a beeline to the top museums and are ready to dig deeper into all the art riches that Amsterdam has to offer. Today you'll have a chance to get off the beaten path to see works unique to this area; contemporary works by local, living artists; and the temporary Stedelijk museum with its incredible collection of modern art. START: **Cobra Museum; tram 5 to Binnenhof or Metro to Beneluxbaan.**

1 ★★ Cobra Museum. Art lovers will find this breathtakingly modern museum worth the trek to its off-the-beaten-path location (I recommend taking a 15-min. taxi ride or 20-min. tram ride straight here and back—it's not the most scenic area of Amsterdam). The museum overflows with the post–World War II abstract expressionist art of the Cobra group, named for the initials of the founding artists' home cities: Copenhagen, Brussels, and Amsterdam. Karel Appel was the Dutchman (born 1921), a controversial painter, sculptor, and graphic artist. As is true of many Cobra artists, Appel's work, including *Child and Beast II* (1951), has a childlike quality, employing bright colors and abstract shapes. He once said, "I paint like a barbarian in a barbarous age." The building's abundant natural light and open space creates a perfect home for the modern art found here. It was designed by Dutch architect Wim Quist (who also designed the Rijksmuseum's south wing). ⏱ *2 hr. If possible, visit on a weekday, when the museum is less crowded. Sandbergplein 1, Amstelveen.* ☎ *020/547-5050. www.cobra-museum.nl. Admission 7€. Tues–Sun 11am–5pm. Tram: 5 to Binnenhof.*

The Cobra Museum's starkly modern interior compliments the art displayed here.

The Hermitage.

② ★★ Hermitage Museum.
Take a taxi or tram back to the center of town to Amsterdam's newest museum, opened in 2004. The Amsterdam branch of Russia's State Hermitage museum of art and fine arts affords you a glimpse into the rich collection previously found only in St. Petersburg. Housed in the neoclassical 1681 Amstelhof (which is flanked on two sides by canals and on a third by the Amstel River), the exhibits here change every 6 months. The Hermitage owns over three million items (of which over 600 are paintings by Dutch and Flemish masters), so you have an excellent chance of seeing some masterpieces on loan from St. Petersburg. A Children's Hermitage is slated to open in 2007. 🕐 *1½ hr. Nieuwe Herengracht 14 (at the Amstel River).* ☎ *020/530-8755. www.hermitage.nl. Admission 6€. Daily 10am–5pm. Tram: 9 or 14 to Waterlooplein.*

③ Sluizer. A few minutes' walk from the Amstel River, you'll find this casual eatery with two dining rooms. One is an old-fashioned brasserie serving simple French fare. The other restaurant serves seafood in an Art Deco dining room, with daily specials ranging from simple cod or eel to scallops and crab casseroles. *Utrechtsestraat 41–43 & 45 (between Herengracht & Keizersgracht).* ☎ *020/622-6376. $$.*

④ Visiting local art galleries.
After leaving the Hermitage, stretch your legs and take in some fresh air as you stroll down the banks of the Amstel River to Kerkastraat (about a 10-min. walk). Turn right on Kerkastraat and you'll find a charming narrow street lined with galleries devoted to contemporary Dutch art. Foremost among them is ArtaCasa (Kerkastraat 411; ☎ 020/639-3213), which changes its exhibits every season. 🕐 *1½ hr. Gallery hours vary, but most are open 1–6pm Tues–Sat.*

⑤ ★★★ Stedelijk CS. The permanent home of the Stedelijk Museum (in the Museumplein) is closed until mid-2006 for major renovations. Until then, you can view a fraction of the museum's stunning collection of modern art at the temporary location close to Centraal Station (hence the CS in the museum's name). Housed in a large, drab-looking building a few minutes' walk from the station, this collection is devoted to post–World War II contemporary art. You'll see works by Karen Appel, Andy Warhol, Willem de Kooning, and Piet Mondrian, among others. The Stedelijk also owns the largest collection (outside of Russia) of the abstract paintings of Kazimir Malevich; three van Goghs: *Montmartre* (1887), *Carnations* (1888), and *The Diggers* (1889); and a small collection of paintings by Chagall, Cezanne, Picasso, and Renoir. Because this space is much smaller than its permanent home, not all the collection is on display, but you can count on seeing examples from the Cobra, post-Cobra, *nouveau realisme,* pop art, color-field painting, zero, minimalist, and conceptual schools of modern art. ⏱ *2 hr. Oosterdokskade 3–5.* ☎ *020/573-2911. www.stedelijk.nl. Admission 7€. Daily 11am–5pm. Tram: 1, 2, 4, 5, 6, 9, 13, 16, 17, 24, or 25 to Centraal Station.*

6⃣ Elf. For an unrivaled ending to your day, head for the top floor of the Stedelijk building and the popular restaurant-cafe-bar Elf (for "11th floor"). There's a sweeping view of Amsterdam, and the space itself is very modern, minimalist, and casual. You'll find good beer and wine selections and satisfying snacks such as the Greek platter with roasted eggplant, feta cheese, olives, and warm pita bread. *11th floor of Oosterdokskade 3–5.* ☎ *020/625-5999. Open daily 11am–11pm. $$.*

Kazimir Malevich's The Floor Polishers.

Architectural Amsterdam

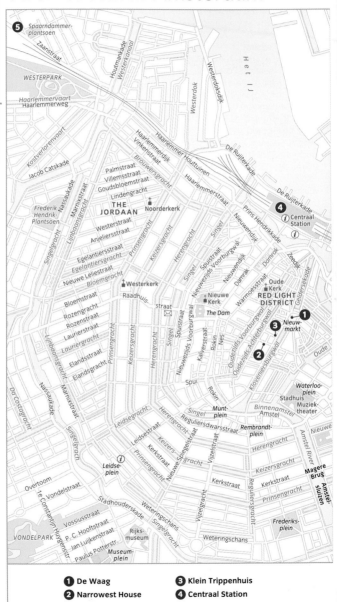

1 De Waag
2 Narrowest House
3 Klein Trippenhuis
4 Centraal Station

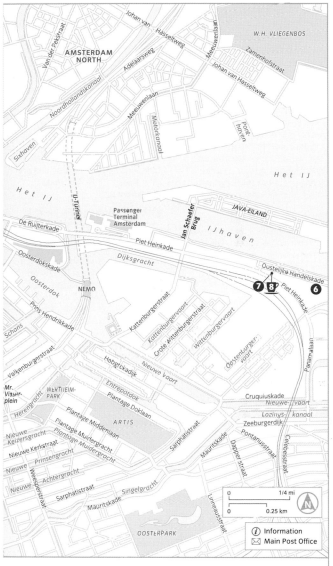

5 Museum Het Schip

6 Lloyd Hotel

7 Panama

8 Panama Restaurant

ⓘ Information

✉ Main Post Office

There are so many architectural styles in Amsterdam that the city can seem quite schizophrenic at times. Architecture buffs can entertain themselves just by walking the streets or taking a tram ride in any corner of the city. On this tour you'll get an overview of the major schools of architecture, starting with medieval, but I've focused on examples from the Amsterdam School, the unique movement that forever changed the look of the city in the early decades of the 20th century. START: **Metro to Nieuwmarkt.**

1 De Waag. On the fringe of what is now the city's Chinatown, you'll find Amsterdam's only surviving medieval fortified gate. Built in the 14th century, it later became a guild house. One of the guilds lodged here was the Surgeon's Guild, immortalized in Rembrandt's painting *The Anatomy Lesson* (1632), which depicts a dissection being conducted in the upper-floor Theatrum Anatomicum. The De Waag is rarely open, but you can meander inside the historic ground-floor restaurant (good international fare, but a bit overpriced—consider just having a cup of coffee) in De Waag. ⏱ *15 min. Nieuwmarkt. Metro: Nieuwmarkt.*

Amsterdam's narrowest house.

2 Narrowest House. Walk toward the Dam to take a look at one of the city's narrowest houses at Oude Hoogstraat 22. The house has a typical Amsterdam bell gable and is only 2m (6½ ft.) wide and 6m (20 ft.) deep. ⏱ *10 min. Oude Hoogstraat 22.*

3 Klein Trippenhuis. Nearby you'll find the cornice-gabled Klein Trippenhuis, also known as Mr. Trip's Coachman's House. This house is only 2.4m (7¾ ft.) wide. It faces the elegant Trippenhuis at no. 29, which at 22m (72 ft.) is the widest Old Amsterdam house, built in 1660 for the wealthy Trip brothers. The story goes that the coachman exclaimed one day: "Oh, if only I could be so lucky as to have a house as wide as my master's door." His master overheard this, and the coachman's wish was granted. The house is now a fashion boutique. ⏱ *10 min. Kloveniersburgwal 26.*

4 Centraal Station. Take a 15-minute walk or jump on any of the trams heading north to Centraal Station, an architectural masterpiece. Designed by architect Petrus Josephus Hubertus Cuypers, it was built between 1884 and 1889 on three artificial islands, which themselves were supported on 30,000 pilings. At the time of its construction, Amsterdammers thoroughly disliked the station, but now the major transportation hub is an attraction in its own right, partly for its extravagant Dutch neo-Renaissance facade and

Centraal Station, Amsterdam's transportation hub.

partly for the liveliness that permanently surrounds it. ⏱ *10 min. Tram: 1, 2, 4, 5, 6, 9, 13, 16, 17, 24, or 25 to Centraal Station.*

❺ **Museum Het Schip.** From Centraal Station, take bus no. 22 heading west (about a 20-min. ride) to the city's most famous example of an Amsterdam School building. The movement's designs, which were influenced by socialist ideas and a reaction to the bourgeois and neo-Gothic architecture of the time, can be recognized by a heavy reliance on brickwork, elaborate masonry, painted glass, and wrought-iron work. Of the dozen or so architects who were part of this school, Michel de Klerk (1884–1923) was the most

Amsterdam's Canal Houses

As you walk around the city's canals, you'll begin to notice that not all canal houses are the same—though they all may look similar. If you look closely, you'll notice a wonderful mix of architectural detail ranging from classical to Renaissance to modern. Most of Amsterdam's 6,800 landmark buildings have gables. These hide the pitched roofs and demonstrate the architect's vertical showmanship in a city where hefty property taxes and expensive canalfront land encouraged pencil-thin buildings.

Around 600 old *gevelstenen* (gable stones)—ornamental tiles, sculptures, or reliefs that often play on the original owner's name or profession—remain. Walls in the Begijnhof and on Sint-Luciënsteeg at the **Amsterdam Historical Museum** (see p 11, bullet ❶) have some good gable stones, including the oldest known (from 1603), showing a milkmaid balancing her buckets.

Incidentally, the *hijsbalk*—the hook you see on many gables—might look to be ideal for a hanging, but it is actually used with rope and pulley for hauling large, heavy items into and out of homes that have steep, narrow staircases.

influential. The museum dedicates itself entirely to the architecture of the Amsterdam School, and is housed in a former post office built in 1919 and designed by de Klerk. The post office was only a small part of this large boatlike building (hence its nickname, "The Ship"): It also contained 102 small homes for the working class. The museum features a very interesting exhibit about the Amsterdam School's sources of inspiration, and explains the social conditions in the Netherlands during World War I that allowed this school of architecture to flourish. A newly restored wing originally housed working-class members of a socialist association in the 1920s and provides an intimate view of the Amsterdam School's unique designs. The renovation boasts original woodwork and colors, plus furniture and utensils identical to the ones used in the '20s—even the closets have been restored to their original style. *Spaarndammerplantsoen 140.* ☎ *20/475-0924. www.hetschip.nl. Admission 5€. Thurs–Sun 1–5pm. Bus: 22 West to Zaanstraat (last stop).*

❻ **Lloyd Hotel.** Hop on the bus back to Centraal Station and connect to bus no. 326 for a quick 8-minute

A window at Museum Het Schip, one of the best examples of the Amsterdam School of architecture.

ride to the East Docklands area, an up-and-coming neighborhood (it's about a 30-min. walk from Centraal Station). Here, old run-down warehouses and large, abandoned historic buildings are being transformed at a maddening pace as the area fills with young professionals scared away by the cramped spaces and high rents in Central Amsterdam. Leave the bus at Rietlandpark and walk across the new park (designed in 2004) to the newly renovated building housing the Lloyd Hotel. This Amsterdam School building was constructed in 1917 and served as a

The Lloyd hotel.

"waiting room" after World War I for immigrant families heading from Eastern Europe to South America. The ground-floor lobby was a high-ceilinged dining room that would seat 350 immigrants. You can walk around these rooms now and take in the stunning renovation, completed in 2004, that transformed this historical space into Amsterdam's most avant-garde hotel (see p 130 for a review of the hotel). During World War II the Germans used this building as a prison, and from 1964 to 1989 it was a detention center for juvenile delinquents. ⊕ *30 min. Oostelijke Handelskade 34. ☎ 020/561-3636. www.lloydhotel.com. Bus: 326. Tram: 10 to Rietlandpark.*

7 ★ **Panama.** Leaving the Lloyd, make a left and walk a few minutes down to the end of the road. Here,

you'll find Club Panama, housed in a former power station built around 1899. Today it's one of the city's trendiest venues, with a happening bar, divine restaurant, and celebrated nightclub (see p 108 for a full review). *Oostelijke Handelskade 4. ☎ 020/311-8686. www.panama.nl. Bus: 326. Tram: 10 to Rietlandpark.*

8 **Panama Restaurant.** Wrap up your tour with a drink in the Panama's fantastic loungelike bar while gazing out floor-to-ceiling windows that overlook the river. The bar has a good selection of appetizers and light meals. You can lounge an afternoon or evening away here, watching the preppy after-work crowd sipping on martinis. *Oostelijke Handelskade 4. ☎ 020/311-8686. $$.*

Urban Minefield

In such a beautiful city, with high gables in many and varied shapes and forms, there's a temptation to walk along gazing upward. Be careful. There's the possibility you'll walk straight into a canal, but that's a minor danger compared to the one underfoot. Many Amsterdammers have dogs, some of them the size of Shetland ponies. Signs on the sidewalk saying HOND IN DE GOOT (DOG IN THE GUTTER) are mostly ignored by both owner and dog. Take your eye off the ground for so much as an instant and you (and your footwear) might regret it.

Amsterdam **with Kids**

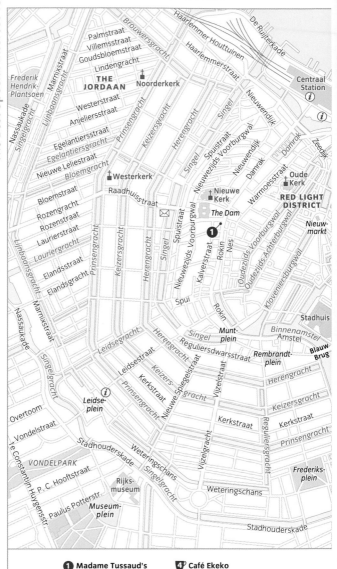

1 Madame Tussaud's   4 Café Ekeko
2 CosmoCafe   5 Tropenmuseum
3 Artis Zoo

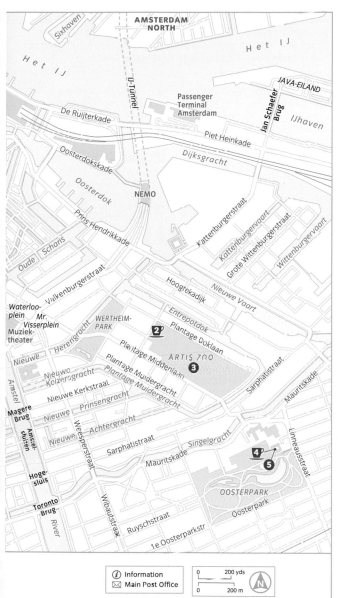

Sixhaven

AMSTERDAM NORTH

H e t   I J

H e t   I J

JAVA-EILAND

IJ-Tunnel

De Ruijterkade

Passenger Terminal Amsterdam

Jan Schaefer Brug

IJhaven

Piet Heinkade

Oosterdokskade

Dijksgracht

Oosterdok

NEMO

Prins Hendrikkade

Kattenburgerstraat

Kattenburgervoort

Grote Wittenburgerstraat

Wittenburgervaart

Oude Schans

Valkenburgerstraat

Hoogtekadijk

Nieuwe Vaart

Waterloo-plein

Mr. Visserplein

Muziek-theater

WERTHEIM-PARK

Herengracht

Entrepotdok

Plantage Doklaan

2

Plantage Middenlaan

ARTIS ZOO

3

Sarphatistraat

Nieuwe

Nieuwe Keizersgracht

Plantage Muidergracht

Plantage Muidergracht

Mauritskade

Nieuwe Kerkstraat

Amstel

Nieuwe Prinsengracht

Nieuwe Achtergracht

Magere Brug

Amstel-sluizen

Nieuwe Weesperstraat

Sarphatistraat

Singelgracht

4

Linnaeusstraat

Hoge-sluis

Mauritskade

5

OOSTERPARK

Toronto Brug

Wibautstraat

Oosterpark

River

Ruyschstraat

1e Oosterparkstr

(i) Information

✉ Main Post Office

| 0 | 200 yds |
| 0 | 200 m |

N

Kids will have plenty to gawk at while walking around Amsterdam—the many houseboats lining the canals and the big barges chugging along the river fascinate children, and a ride on a tram can be an attraction in itself. You may also want to take them on the Maritime City tour (later in this chapter), especially if they're over 5. START: **Tram, 4, 9, 14, 16, 24, or 25 to the Dam.**

1 ★★ Madame Tussauds. Spend a frivolous morning at this popular museum. You'll see all the waxen celebrities you'd expect, plus the many hands-on activities that make this museum a winner for kids. In the "Be the Next Idol" exhibit, modeled after the popular TV show, you sing a tune of your choice and hear what the jury says about you. In the Royalty section, kids can wear tiaras and crowns and have their pictures taken with a wax Queen Beatrix. As you walk around, you'll see celebs from all eras and walks of life, from Charlie Chaplin, Picasso, van Gogh, and Marilyn Monroe to George W. Bush, Nelson Mandela, Madonna, and Harrison Ford as Indiana Jones. ⏱ *2 hr. Arrive right at opening time to avoid the crowds. Dam 20.* ☎ *020/522-1010. www. madametussauds.nl. Admission 23€; 18€ children 5–16; free for children under 5. Mid-July to mid-Aug*

daily 10am–11pm; mid-Aug to mid-July daily 10am–6:30pm. Closed Apr 30. Tram: 4, 9, 14, 16, 24, or 25 to the Dam.

2 CosmoCafe. If it's a nice day and you're headed to the zoo, fuel up for your visit by taking a break at this fun eatery located inside the planetarium, near the entrance. Fill up on tasty sandwiches and other snacks while looking at the stars and planets. There's also a video arcade. *Inside Artis Zoo Planetarium.* ☎ *020/523-3400. $.*

3 ★★★ Artis Zoo. Head here if it's a nice day; if not, skip this stop and go to Café Ekeko (next stop) for lunch, then the Tropenmuseum (stop no. 5) instead. Amsterdam's oldest city park houses this fantastic zoo, established in 1838. It's huge— over 14 hectares (34 acres)—so I

Seals at the Artis Zoo.

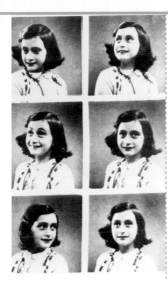

These photos of Anne Frank were taken around 1940.

suggest buying a map at the entrance and targeting the animals your kids want to see most. There are two restaurants and several cafes to choose from, making it easy to spend the whole day here. There are over 6,000 animals and 1,400 species. You can spot giraffes at the African Savannah and llamas and guanacos in the South American Pampas. There's an aquarium (built in 1882 and renovated in 1996), a planetarium, the Insect House, and the Geological Museum. There's also a children's farm, where kids can pet assorted Dutch animals. Most kids love the chimpanzees; the zoo rotates the animals on display so they—the animals, that is—never seem tired or bored with the visiting throngs. Try to catch one of these daily feedings: The European vultures are fed at 11am, sea lions at

"A Voice within Me Is Sobbing"

The handsome merchant house where the Frank family lived faces one of the city's most charming canals. The house was built in 1653 and doubled as a warehouse. Otto Frank, who moved his family here from Frankfurt, Germany, in 1933, stored his herbs and spices in the front of the house. The back, known as the Secret Annex, later became the family's hiding place. For 25 months, the Frank family (father Otto, his wife Edith, and their two daughters Margot and Anne) and four family friends hid from Nazi invaders. The hideaway was concealed from the front of the house by a moveable bookcase. Anne began writing in her diary on her birthday, June 12, 1942. Her last entry was on August 1, 1944, shortly before Nazi officers stormed the hideaway and the family was sent to separate concentration camps. Anne Frank died at Bergen-Belsen concentration camp from a typhus epidemic. Only Otto survived the camps. He returned to the house after the war and fulfilled Anne's wishes to have her diary published. The first edition, in Dutch, appeared in 1947. Since then, Anne's diary has been published in over 60 languages.

Older children, especially those who have read *The Diary of Anne Frank*, will be interested in seeing the house where Anne and her family hid for 2 harrowing years. For information on visiting the Anne Frankhuis, see p 9, bullet **6**.

Kids may not appreciate NeMO's unique architecture, but they're sure to enjoy the hands-on exhibits inside.

11:30am and 3:45pm, pelicans at 2:30pm, and penguins at 3:30pm. Crocodiles are fed on Sunday only at 2:30pm. ⏲ *3–5 hr. Plantage Kerklaan 38–40 (at Plantage Middenlaan).* ☎ *020/523-3400. www.artis.nl. Admission 15€; 11€ children 3–9; free for children under 3. July–Aug daily 9am–6pm (Sat to 10pm); Sept–June daily 9am–5pm. Tram: 9 or 14 to Plantage Kerklaan; 6 to Plantage Doklaan.*

4 Café Ekeko. Adjacent to the Tropenmuseum Junior, this lively cafe is a perfect place to sample a drink and a meal or snack from one of the tropical countries you're about to visit. The changing menu might include such specialties as vegetable samosas from India, a Thai beef salad, or Caribbean chicken with rice. *Inside the Tropenmuseum. $.*

5 ★★ Tropenmuseum (Tropical Museum). The Royal Institute for the Tropics owns this unusual museum devoted to the study of the cultures of tropical areas around the world. Its focus reflects Holland's former role as a landlord in such countries as Indonesia, Surinam, and the Caribbean islands of St.

Maarten, Bonaire, and Aruba. The building itself is noteworthy for its heavily ornamented 19th-century facade featuring turrets, stepped gables, arched windows, and delicate spires, and a monumental galleried interior court. Of the exhibits, the most fascinating for kids are the walk-through model villages and city-street scenes that capture a moment in daily life. You can stroll through a Nigerian village, an Arab

The Tropenmuseum has a special section just for kids.

souk, and a traditional yurt tent home of nomads in central Asia. You'll also see fantastic wedding costumes from Thailand and Turkey and bridal jewelry from Northern Sumatra. In the Tropenmuseum Junior, kids learn about tropical countries and their people through stories, dances, games, and paintings. This part of the museum is only open to children ages 6 to 12 (and one adult per child). The Tropenmuseum Junior opens on Wednesday, Saturday, Sunday, national holidays, and during all school holidays. ⏰ *2 hr. Linnaeusstraat 2 (at Mauritskade).* ☎ *020/658-8215. www.tropen museum.nl. Admission 7.50€; 3.75€ children 6–17; free for children under 6. Daily 10am–5pm (3pm Dec 5, 24, 31). Closed Jan 1, Apr 30, May 5, Dec 25. Tram: 7, 9, 10, or 14 to Mauritskade.*

Another Rainy-Day Option

If you find yourself with a rainy afternoon and stir-crazy kids on your hands, head to **NeMO** (Oosterdok 2, off Prins Hendrikkade, over the south entrance to the IJ Tunnel; ☎ 0900/919-1100; www.nemo.nl). This swooping, modern building, designed by Italian architect Renzo Piano, looks like a graceful oceangoing ship. NeMO is as much a hands-on experience as it is a museum, as evidenced by its motto: "Forbidden Not to Touch." Through games, experiments, and demonstrations, kids learn how to steer a supertanker safely into port, execute a complicated surgical procedure, blow a soap bubble large enough to stand inside, and more. Exhibits answer questions like: Why is water clear but the ocean blue? Why does toothpaste contain sugar? In Istudio Bis & Co, NeMO's digital world, you can don a virtual-reality helmet and play with images, sounds, and websites. The broad, sloping stairway to NeMO's roof is an attraction in itself, a place to hang out and take in the magnificent views. At the top, you are 30m (98 ft.) above the IJ channel and have sweeping views over the Old Harbor and Eastern Dock. This museum is great for kids 9 or older. Admission is 11€; children under 4 are free. It's open daily from 10am to 5pm July and August; Tuesday to Sunday from 10am to 5pm September through June. The museum is closed January 1, April 30, and December 25.

Maritime Amsterdam

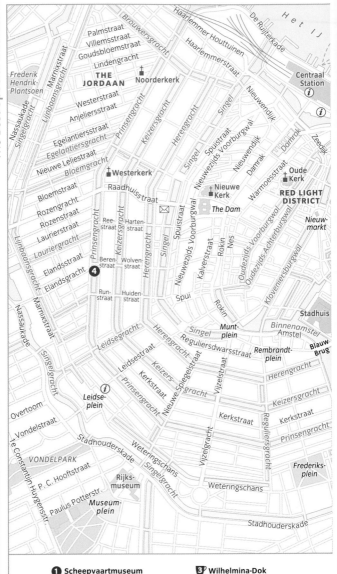

Het IJ

De Ruijterkade

Haarlemmer Houttuinen

Brouwersgracht

Haarlemmerstraat

Palmstraat

Villemsstraat

Goudsbloemstraat

Lindengracht

Centraal
Station
ⓘ

THE
JORDAAN

Noorderkerk

Frederik-
Hendrik-
Plantsoen

Nassaukade

Singelgracht

Marnixstraat

Lijnbaansgracht

Westerstraat

Anjeliersstraat

Egelantiersstraat

Egelantiersgracht

Nieuwe Leliestraat

Bloemgracht

Prinsengracht

Keizersgracht

Herengracht

Singel

Singel

Nieuwendijk

ⓘ

Singel

Spuistraat

Nieuwezijds Voorburgwal

Nieuwendijk

Damrak

Damrak

Zeedijk

Warmoesstraat

Oude
Kerk

RED LIGHT
DISTRICT

Westerkerk

Raadhuisstraat

Nieuwe
Kerk

The Dam

✉

Nieuw-
markt

Bloemstraat

Rozengracht

Rozenstraat

Laurierstraat

Lauriergracht

Elandsstraat

Elandsgracht

Lijnbaansgracht

Marnixstraat

Prinsengracht

Keizersgracht

Ree-
straat

Harten-
straat

Beren-
straat

Wolven-
straat

Herengracht

Singel

Nieuwezijds Voorburgwal

Spuistraat

Kalverstraat

Rokin

Nes

Oudezijds Voorburgwal

Oudezijds Achterburgwal

Klovenniersburgwal

4

Run-
straat

Huiden-
straat

Spui

Rokin

Stadhuis

Nassaukade

Singelgracht

Leidsegracht

Leidsestraat

Keizers-
gracht

Herengracht

Reguliersdwarsstraat

Singel

Munt-
plein

Binnenamstel

Amstel

Blauw
Brug

Rembrandt-
plein

Herengracht

Kerkstraat

Nieuwe Spiegelstraat

Prinsengracht

Vizelstraat

Keizersgracht

ⓘ

Leidse-
plein

Overtoom

Vondelstraat

Stadhouderskade

Weteringschans

Singelgracht

Vijzelgracht

Kerkstraat

Reguliersgracht

Kerkstraat

Prinsengracht

VONDELPARK

1e Constantijn Huygensstr.

P. C. Hooftstraat

Paulus Potterstr.

Rijks-
museum

Museum-
plein

Weteringschans

Weteringschans

Frederiks-
plein

Stadhouderskade

❶ Scheepvaartmuseum

❷ Ferry to North Amsterdam

❸ Wilhelmina-Dok

❹ Houseboat Museum

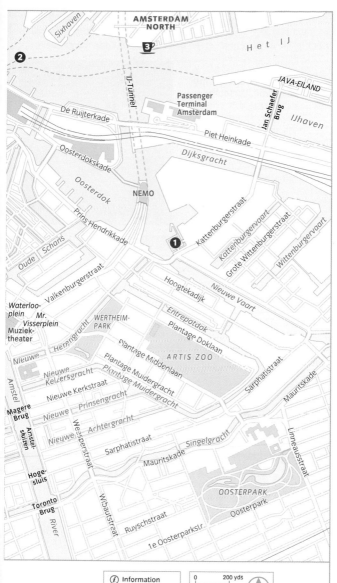

AMSTERDAM
NORTH

Het IJ

Sixhaven

JAVA-EILAND

IJ-Tunnel

De Ruijterkade

Passenger
Terminal
Amsterdam

Jan Schaefer
Brug

IJhaven

Piet Heinkade

Oosterdokskade

Dijksgracht

Oosterdok

Oosterdok

NEMO

Prins Hendrikkade

Kattenburgerstraat

Kattenburgervaart

Grote Wittenburgerstraat

Wittenburgervaart

Oude Schans

Valkenburgerstraat

Hoogtekadijk

Nieuwe Vaart

Waterloo-
plein

Mr.
Visserplein

Muziek-
theater

WERTHEIM-
PARK

Entrepotdok

Plantage Doklaan

Herengracht

Plantage Middenlaan

ARTIS ZOO

Nieuwe

Nieuwe
Keizersgracht

Plantage Muidergracht

Plantage Muidergracht

Sarphatistraat

Mauritskade

Nieuwe Kerkstraat

Amstel

Nieuwe Prinsengracht

Achtergracht

Magere
Brug

Nieuwe

Wesperstraat

Sarphatistraat

Mauritskade

Singelgracht

Linnaeusstraat

Amstel-
sluizen

Hoge-
sluis

Wibautstraat

OOSTERPARK

Oosterpark

Toronto
Brug

River

Ruyschstraat

1e Oosterparkstr.

(i) Information

✉ Main Post Office

| 0 | 200 yds |
| 0 | 200 m |

N

Holland's history and culture are inextricably linked to the sea, as you'll discover for yourself on a maritime tour of Amsterdam. This tour takes you to one of the country's best maritime museums, guides you across the river on a ferry, and then lets you peek inside a houseboat. START: **Bus 22 or 32 to Kattenburgerplein.**

1 ★★★ kids **Scheepvaart-museum (Maritime Museum).**
This gem of a museum overlooks the busy harbor. Moored on the wharf is the museum's main attraction: an immense replica of the V.O.C. merchant ship *Amsterdam,* which foundered off Hastings, England, in 1749 on her maiden voyage to Indonesia. You can climb aboard and explore every nook and cranny. Re-enactors create scenes from everyday life on the ship. Sailors fire cannons, sing sea shanties, mop the deck, hoist cargo on board, and attend a solemn "burial at sea." You can watch sailmakers and rope-makers at work and see the cook prepare a shipboard meal in the galley. Inside the grand museum, gems include the Royal Barge, used by the monarchy from 1818 to 1982. Room after room is filled with boats and ship models, paintings and prints of ships, seascapes, navigational instruments, cannons and other weaponry, and old maps and charts. Among the important papers on display are several pertaining to the Dutch

A boy gets a close-up look at a cannon at the Maritime Museum.

colonies of Nieuw Amsterdam (New York) and Nieuw Nederland (New York State), including a receipt for the land that now surrounds the New York State capital at Albany. ⏱ *3 hr. Kattenburgerplein 1 (in the Eastern Dock).* ☎ *020/523-2222. www.scheepvaartmuseum.nl. Admission 7.50€; 4€ children 6–17; free for children under 6. Tues–Sat 10am–5pm (also Mon during school vacations); Sun noon–5pm. Bus: 22 or 32 to Kattenburgerplein.*

The merchant ship Amsterdam.

The Houseboat Museum.

2 ★★ kids **Crossing the River to North Amsterdam.** Take this free ferry ride across the river to see the city and its numerous boats up close. From Pier 8, just behind Centraal Station, IJveer ferries leave every 10 to 15 minutes. 🕐 *10-min. crossing.*

3 ★★ kids **Wilhelmina-Dok.** With its fantastic glass-walled terrace right on the river, this fun cafe/restaurant boasts incredible views of the boats and the cruise-ship terminal on the south shore. Organic salads and delicious sandwiches are the specialties here; if you're eager to continue your maritime experience with a seafood dish, the grilled swordfish with saffron rice is your best bet. *Nordwal 1 (at IJplein).* ☎ 020/632-3701. $$.

4 ★ kids **Houseboat Museum.** Take the ferry back to Centraal Station and jump on the tram to get to this houseboat moored on the edge of the Jordaan. Over 2,400 private houseboats float peacefully on the canals of Amsterdam; this museum gives you an intriguing look inside a particularly well-preserved example. Inside the *Hendrika Maria,* a former commercial sailing vessel built in 1914, you can visit the original deckhouse where the skipper and his family lived. The cupboard bed and the comfortable living quarters are yours to explore. Kids will enjoy the small play area devoted to them. There are plenty of interesting photographs and books relating to houseboats. 🕐 *30 min. Opposite Prinsengracht 296 (near Elandsgracht).* ☎ *020/427-0750. www. houseboatmuseum.nl. Admission 3€; 2.25€ children under 152cm (59 in.). Mar–Oct Tues–Sun 11am–5pm; Nov–Feb Fri–Sun 11am–5pm. Closed Jan 1, Apr 30, Dec 25, 26, 27. Tram: 6, 13, 14, or 17 to Westermarkt.*

Alternative Amsterdam

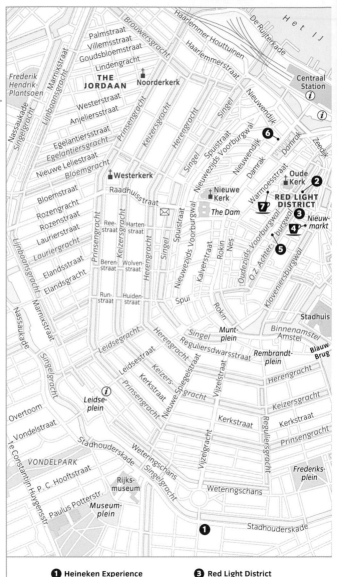

1 Heineken Experience

2 Erotic Museum

3 Red Light District

4 't Loosje

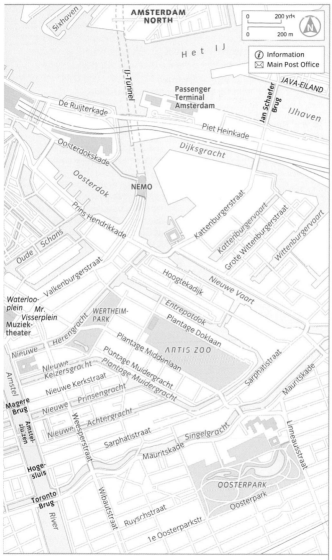

5 Hash Marihuana Hemp Museum

6 Sexmuseum Amsterdam

7 Winston International

Amsterdam has a reputation for being a wild party town with tolerant attitudes toward many aspects of life. Not only is it one of the biggest producers of beer in the world, Amsterdam tolerates the growing and selling of cannabis in small amounts, and Dutch law allows prostitution. The Red Light District is known the world over for its scantily clad women luring customers from behind glass windows. This tour will give you a chance to discover the wilder side of Amsterdam, but not surprisingly, your day may not end until well after midnight. START: **Tram 16, 24, or 25 to Stadhouderskade.**

1 ★★ Heineken Experience. This place is usually a hit with a 20-something (mostly male) crowd who enjoy the two free beers (and a free Heineken glass as a souvenir) as much as they enjoy the myriad rides and shows. It's a hoot if you just get loose and go with the flow—and you'll learn a few things about beer while you're at it. It's housed inside the former working brewery (built around 1867), but the operation moved out of this facility in 1988. Now it's sort of a mini-Disneyland built around historic machinery. The fermentation tanks, each capable of holding a million glasses of Heineken, are still here, along with the multi-story malt silos and all manner of vintage brewing equipment and implements. In one amusing attraction, you stand on a moving floor, facing a large video screen, and get to see and feel what it's like to be a Heineken beer bottle careening on a conveyor belt—one of a half million every hour—through a modern Heineken plant. ⏱ *2 hr. Stadhouderskade 78 (at Ferdinand Bolstraat).* ☎ *020/523-9666. www.heinekenexperience.com. Admission 10€ (includes 2 beers). Tues–Sun 10am–6pm. Closed Jan 1, Dec 25. Tram: 16, 24, or 25 to Stadhouderskade.*

2 Erotic Museum. Spread over five floors, this wacky place boasts many provocative prints and drawings, including some by John Lennon. More interesting is a re-creation of a red-light alley and an extensively

Copper brewing kettles at the Heineken Experience.

The Erotic Museum is just one of Amsterdam's sex-themed museums.

equipped S&M playroom. Don't miss the X-rated cartoon depicting some of the things Snow White apparently got up to with the Seven Dwarfs that we were never told about as kids!
⏲ 45 min. *Oudezijds Achterburgwal 54.* ☎ *020/624-7303. Admission 5€. Sun–Thurs 11am–1am; Fri–Sat 11am–2am. Tram: 4, 9, 14, 16, 24, or 25 to the Dam.*

❸ **Red Light District.** Upon leaving the Erotic Museum, you'll find yourself in the Red Light District. If you take a peek down any of the tiny alleyways, you'll see the prostitutes hanging out behind their windows waiting for customers. Some may be on cellphones, some may be knitting. Many will be in various stages of undress (though never fully naked). If the curtains are closed, then you know that a deal has been . . . consummated. Probably what you'll notice most of all are the throngs of testosterone-driven men circling these tiny alleyways with hungry eyes. It's not dangerous here, just a bit seedy, though you shouldn't take photos at any time;

it's best to hide your camera when you stroll here, especially at night. Early evening is the best time to visit, before it gets crowded but late enough that you can see the red lights reflecting off the canals.
⏲ 30 min. *Along Oudezijds Achterburgwal & the tiny alleyways that intersect it.*

❹ **'t Loosje.** Steps from the Red Light District (toward Nieuwmarkt) is a busy, friendly brown cafe that was built in 1900. Tiles from that period still ornament the walls. It's a great place to people-watch. Many beers are on tap, and they have a good choice of snacks. Try the Dutch croquettes or *bitterballen* (fried minced-meat-and-potato balls) dipped in hot mustard. *Nieuwmarkt 32–34.* ☎ *020/623-4419. $.*

❺ ★ **Hash Marihuana Hemp Museum.** Only in Amsterdam, eh? This museum will teach you everything you wanted to know about hash, marijuana, and related products. The museum does not promote

You can find prostitutes waiting for customers around the clock in the Red Light District.

drug use; instead it aims to make you better informed. There's a cannabis garden where you can see plants at various stages of development. Some exhibits shed light on the medicinal use of cannabis and on hemp's past and present-day uses as a natural fiber. ⏱ *1 hr. Oudezijds Achterburgwal 130 (Red Light District).* ☎ *020/623-5961. www.hashmuseum.com. Admission 5.70€. Daily 11am–11pm. Closed Jan 1, Apr 30, Dec 25. Tram: 4, 9, 14, 16, 24, or 25 to the Dam.*

⑥ Sexmuseum Amsterdam.
For more of Amsterdam's wild side, head over to this unique museum More than half a million visitors traipse through here every year to learn more about the history of sex. Teenagers end up giggling quite a bit. "Sex through the ages and cultures" is the theme of one exhibit, which includes such 19th-century erotic objects as a fragment of a Delft blue tile showing a man with an erection playing cards. There's an interesting exhibit about early erotic photography and many erotic prints and drawings and trinkets decorated

The Sexmuseum, another of Amsterdam's sex-themed museums.

with naughty pictures. It's open late, so you can come here after dark, before you head out to the club below. ⏱ *1 hr. Damrak 18 (near Centraal Station).* ☎ *020/622-8376. www.sexmuseumamsterdam.com. Admission 2.50€. Daily 10am–11:30pm. Tram: 1, 2, 4, 5, 9, 13, 16, 17, 24, or 25 to Centraal Station.*

⑦ ★ Winston International. End your day at this very happening and very fun venue inside the Winston Hotel at the edge of the Red Light District. You'll find live music, drag shows, singalongs, and other shows every night of the week in this small, intimate space with a very eclectic, live-and-let-live, quintessentially Amsterdam crowd. The dress code is suave, sexy, and glamorous, but basically anything goes as long as you're having a good time. There are light snacks and drinks, and the cover ranges between 5€ and 7€. Things really get going after 10pm. *Winston Hotel, Warmoesstraat 125.* ☎ *020/623-1380.* ●

Learn the history of cannabis at the Hash Marijuana Hemp Museum.

3 The Best
Neighborhood Walks

Golden Age **Canals**

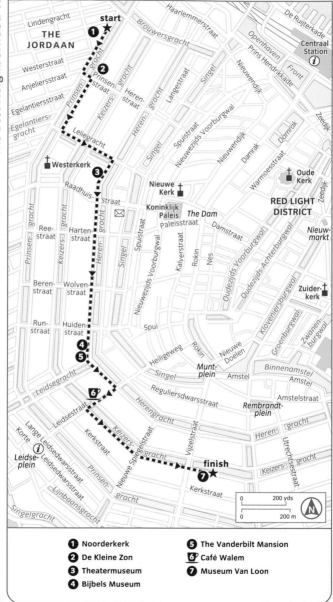

1 Noorderkerk
2 De Kleine Zon
3 Theatermuseum
4 Bijbels Museum
5 The Vanderbilt Mansion
6 Café Walem
7 Museum Van Loon

Amsterdam's glory days date back to the 17th century, a time known as "The Golden Age." This tour will give you an in-depth view of the brilliant architecture of that time as you pass innumerable canal houses with gables in various styles (bell, step, neck, and variations), as well as a peek into hidden almshouses and courtyards and the opportunity to visit three important museums. START: **Tram: 1, 2, 5, 13, or 17 to Martelaarsgracht.**

❶ ★★ Noorderkerk. The North Church was the last masterpiece by architect Hendrick de Keyser, the guiding hand behind many of Amsterdam's historic churches. Dating back to 1623, it was built for the poor Calvinist faithful of the Jordaan nearby. It was recently restored and today has an active congregation. From May to September a classical-music recital takes place here every Saturday at 2pm; admission is 5€. The Noordermarkt square, where the church is located, hosts a Saturday farmers market with organic products for sale from 10am to 3pm. ⏱ *30 min. Noordermarkt 44–48 (at Prinsengracht).* ☎ *020/626-6436. Free admission. Mon 10:30am– 12:30pm; Sat 11am–1pm; Sun (services) 10am & 7pm.*

❷ De Kleine Zon. Walk up Prinsengracht to no. 159, where you'll find a hidden almshouse surrounding a courtyard garden at the end of a long passageway. Almshouses (or *hofjes*) are like a cloister, and always have a garden in the middle. They were built by wealthy citizens starting in the 14th century for the old and needy; they were also inhabited by pious women. Today, students, seniors, and people who may need assisted living reside in almshouses. At De Kleine Zon, the outer door is open from 10am to 5pm Monday through Saturday, and you can walk quietly through the passageway to the courtyard, which belonged to the city's Mennonites. They held meetings in this serene courtyard, which they called *De Kleine Zon* (The Little Sun). This is a great place for a moment of contemplation, away from the bustle of the city. *159 Prinsengracht.*

The interior of North Church.

3 ★ **Theatermuseum.** Back on Prinsengracht, turn left along the picturesque Leliegracht canal, then right onto Herengracht, the ultimate Amsterdam address for flourishing bankers and merchants in the 17th century. At no. 168 is the Theatermuseum, known as the Het Witte Huis (the White House) for its whitish-gray, neoclassical sandstone facade. This graceful house was built in 1638 for Michiel Pauw, who established a short-lived trading colony in America at Hoboken, New Jersey. Dazzling interior ornamentation from around 1730 includes a spiral staircase, intricate stuccowork, and painted ceilings by Jacob de Wit. The museum extends into the flamboyant Bartolotti House (nos. 170–172), built in 1617 for Guillielmo Bartolotti. Bartolotti began life as Willem van den Heuvel and switched to the fancier moniker after he made his bundle in brewing and banking. In the museum you'll find costumes, masks, puppets, photos, miniature theaters, and backdrops. Hands-on exhibits let you create your own stage and sound effects. 🕐 *1 hr. Herengracht 168.* ☎ *020/551-3300. www.tin.nl. Admission 4.50€. Mon–Fri 11am–5pm; Sat–Sun 1–5pm.*

4 **Bijbels Museum (Biblical Museum).** Stroll down Herengracht, taking in the view of the canals and canal houses with their varied gables. Two of a group of four 1660s houses (nos. 364–370) with delicate neck gables house the Biblical Museum. The houses were designed by architect Philips Vingboons for timber merchant Jacob Cromhout, and are known as the Cromhouthuizen or as the "Father, Mother, and Twins." The museum itself features Bibles and things biblical, buts its canal-house setting with its elegant stucco decoration, dizzying elliptical staircase, and illuminated ceilings by Jacob de

Wit are worth the admission price alone. 🕐 *1 hr. Herengracht 366–368.* ☎ *020/624-2436. www.bijbels museum.nl. Admission 6€. Mon–Sat 10am–5pm; Sun & holidays 11–5pm.*

5 **The Vanderbilt Mansion.** A few steps down Herengracht bring you to this replica of the elaborate Loire chateau–style Fifth Avenue mansion (at nos. 380–382) built for U.S. tycoon William H. Vanderbilt in New York. Constructed in 1890 for Dutch tobacco merchant Jacob Nienhuys, it now houses the Netherlands Institute for War Documentation (not open to visitors). Across the canal, on the facade of Herengracht 395, a stone cat stalks its prey—a carved mouse on the facade of the neighboring house, no. 397 (it's not easy to see unless you cross over tiny Beulingluis canal for a close-up look). *Herengracht 380–382.*

6 ★★ **Café Walem.** Cross elegant Leidsegracht (dug in 1664 for barge traffic) and walk along Leidsestraat to its junction with Keizersgracht. The Walem, designed by Philippe Starck, is a trendy cafe/restaurant

The Biblical Museum

with two wonderful terraces (one outside beside the canal and the other at the rear in a sheltered and quiet garden patio). The home-smoked-salmon sandwich on fresh farm bread with chives, crème fraîche, and cucumbers is exquisite. *Keizersgracht 449.* ☎ *020/625-3544. $$.*

A room inside the richly decorated Museum Van Loon.

⑦ ★★★ Museum Van Loon.
Continue down Keizersgracht to yet another magnificent canal house, this one dating back to 1672. Its first occupant was the artist Ferdinand Bol, a student of Rembrandt. The elegant home was owned by the Van Loon family from 1884 to 1945. On its walls hang more than 80 family portraits, including those of Willem van Loon, one of the founders of the Dutch United East India Company. A marble staircase with an ornately curlicued brass balustrade leads up through the house, connecting restored period rooms that are filled with richly decorated paneling, stuccowork, mirrors, fireplaces, furnishings, porcelain, medallions, chandeliers, rugs, and more. Be sure to look out into the garden at the carefully tended hedges and the coach house modeled on a Greek temple. ◷ *1 hr. Keizersgracht 672.* ☎ *020/624-5255. www.museumvanloon.nl. Admission 5€. Sept–June Fri–Mon 11am–5pm; July–Aug daily 11am–5pm.*

Gables 101

Most of Amsterdam's 6,800 landmark buildings have gables. These hide the pitched roofs and demonstrate the architect's vertical showmanship in a city where hefty property taxes and expensive canalfront land encouraged pencil-thin buildings. If you can pick out Amsterdam's various gable styles without developing Sistine Chapel–neck syndrome, you can date the buildings fairly accurately. Of the earliest, triangular wood gables (1250–1550) only two remain, at no. 34 in the Begijnhof and at Zeedijk 1. Later developments in stone on this theme (1600–50) were the pointy spout gable and the step gable, which, as the name suggests, looks like a series of steps. The graceful neck gable (1640–1790) looks like a headless neck, with curlicues on the shoulders.

The Jordaan

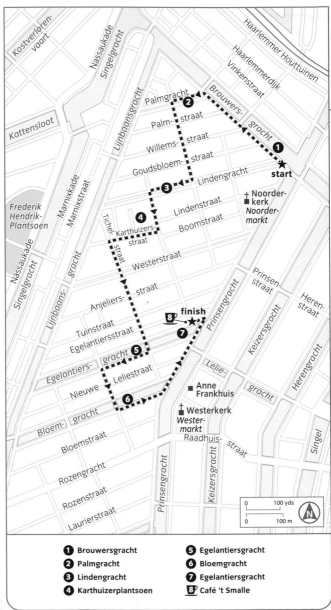

1. Brouwersgracht
2. Palmgracht
3. Lindengracht
4. Karthuizerplantsoen
5. Egelantiersgracht
6. Bloemgracht
7. Egelantiersgracht
8. Café 't Smalle

The Jordaan is one of Amsterdam's most elegant neighborhoods, where many of the city's more successful artists, intellectuals, and slightly older yuppies reside. Among the district's charms are tiny canals, lovely bridges, and several of the delightful, centuries-old almshouses called *hofjes*. If you enter these courtyards, tread softly—people live here. This walk can be taken at any time, though the late afternoon on a warm day would be best so you can end at a canalside cafe. START: **Tram 1, 2, 4, 5, 6, 7, 9, 12, 24, or 25 to Centraal Station, then a 10-minute walk to Brouwersgracht.**

---

❶ ★ Brouwersgracht. Stroll along this lovely houseboat-lined canal and cross Lindengracht. You'll pass a bronze sculpture from 1979 of Jordaan schoolchild Kees de Jongen, a popular fictional character of Dutch writer Theo Thijssen (1879–1943). Keep going until you cross Willemstraat, then look across the water for a wide view of the modern De Blauwe Burgt apartment block (you can cross over on the Oranjebrug bridge for a close-up look). It's a good example of the new architecture mixed with the old.

❷ Palmgracht. Turn left onto this tree-shaded street, which was once a canal. The house at nos. 28–38 hides a small cobblestone courtyard garden behind an orange door that's the entrance to the Raepenhofje, an almshouse from 1648. If you're lucky, the door will be open and you can peek into the courtyard. *Palmgracht 28–38.*

❸ Lindengracht. Turn left on Palmdwarsstraat and cross over Willemstraat (which used to be a canal known as Goudsbloemgracht) into Tweede Goudsbloemdwarsstraat. Cross over Goudsbloemstraat to Lindengracht. This was once the Jordaan's most important canal and is now the scene of a lively Saturday street market. The 15 small houses (originally there were 19) of the pretty Suyckerhoff Hofje, at Lindengracht 149–163, were built in 1670 as a refuge for Protestant widows and for women of good moral standing and a "tranquil character," who had been abandoned by their husbands. The door may be closed but you can generally open it during daylight hours and walk along the narrow entrance corridor to a courtyard garden filled with flowers and plants. *Lindengracht 149–163.*

One of Brouwersgracht's houseboats.

One of Egelantiersgracht's cafes.

4 Karthuizerplantsoen. From Lindengracht, turn left onto Tweede Lindendwarsstraat. Nothing is left of the Carthusian monastery from 1394 that once stretched from here to Lijnbaansgracht (the monastery was destroyed in the 1570s). A playground marks the spot where its cemetery stood. At Karthuizerstraat 11–19 is a row of neck-gabled houses from 1737, named after the four seasons: Lente, Zomer, Herfst, and Winter (spring, summer, fall,

Bloemgracht.

winter). Next door, at nos. 69–191, is the Huyszitten-Weduwenhof, which dates from 1650 and used to shelter poor widows. Today students live in these houses, which surround a large interior courtyard. *Karthuizerstraat 11–191.*

5 ★★★ Egelantiersgracht. Hang a left on Tichelstraat to reach the Egelantiersgracht. As you make your way here, you'll notice the tall spire of the Westerkerk. Named for the eglantine rose, or sweetbrier, Egelantiersgracht is one of the city's most picturesque and tranquil small canals and is lined with 17th- and 18th-century houses. This is where successful Amsterdam artisans lived in the 17th century. If the door is open, take a peek into the Andrieshofje at nos. 107–145. Cattle farmer Ivo Gerrittsszoon financed this almshouse of 36 houses, which was completed in 1617 and remodeled in 1884. A corridor decorated with Delft blue tiles leads up to a small courtyard with a manicured garden. *107–145 Egelantiersgracht.*

6 Bloemgracht. The grandest of the Jordaan canals, Bloemgracht originally was home to workers who produced dyes and paints. The three step-gabled houses at nos. 87–91 were built in 1642 by architect

Egelantiersgracht.

Hendrick de Keyser and now house a foundation established to preserve his work. Their carved gable stones represent a townsman, a country-man, and a seaman. Nos. 77 and 81 are two former sugar refineries from 1752 and 1763.

7 Egelantiersgracht. Make a left on Prinsengracht and you'll find yourself back at Egelantiersgracht. The hardware store at nos. 2–6, at the corner of Prinsengracht, is a fine example of an Amsterdam School of Architecture design from 1917. Its intricate brickwork and cast-iron ornaments were influenced by Art Deco. To the left of the store, at no. 8, a step-gabled house from 1649 is decorated with sandstone orna-ments and gable stones that depict St. Willibrord and a brewer.

8 ★★ Café 't Smalle. With its lovely terrace, this cafe is one of the best in the Jordaan for a drink and a typical Dutch snack of *bitterballen* (fried minced-meat-and-potato balls), chunks of Gouda dipped in mustard, or homemade pea soup. *Egelantiersgracht 12.* ☎ *020/623-9617. $.*

Walking Tour Tips

Allow between 2 and 2½ hours for walking around the Jordaan. If you want to visit one of this neighborhood's lively markets, go either on a Monday morning or on Saturday. On Monday, there's a flea mar-ket on Noordermarkt and a textiles market on Westerstraat where you find, among other items, fabrics, and secondhand clothing. On Saturday, Noordermarkt hosts a bird market and a farmers market that has organically grown produce, and Lindengracht has a general street market. For more on shopping in this area, see chapter 4.

The Jewish Quarter

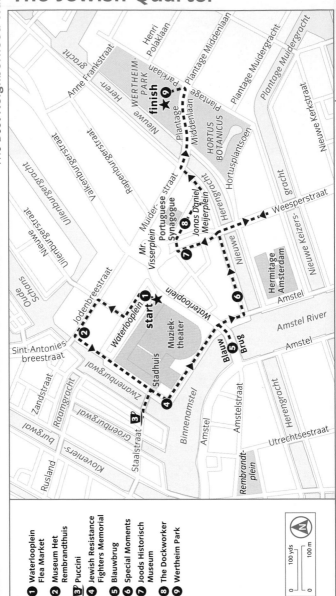

1 Waterlooplein Flea Market
2 Museum Het Rembrandthuis
3 Puccini
4 Jewish Resistance Fighters Memorial
5 Blauwbrug
6 Special Moments
7 Joods Historisch Museum
8 The Dockworker
9 Wertheim Park

start 1

finish 9

100 yds
100 m

This historical area, just to the east of the Old Center, used to be Amsterdam's main Jewish neighborhood. It has changed almost beyond recognition since World War II, but there remain mementos and memorials of Amsterdam's once-thriving Jewish community. It's a great area for a stroll, starting with the city's most popular flea market near the Muziektheater (the home of the Netherlands Opera and Ballet) and Town Hall, and ending with the rich Jewish Historical Museum. START: Tram 9 or 14 to Waterlooplein.

❶ ★ Waterlooplein Flea Market. The most popular flea market in Amsterdam sells everything from sweaters, hats, and gloves to CDs, books, and faux Rembrandt paintings. You'll also find stalls selling raw herring and herring sandwiches. If you're feeling adventurous, try a local favorite: a herring sandwich with pickles and raw onion. In the passageway between the Muziektheater and the Town Hall, you'll see three glass columns filled with water. This is the NAP, Normaal Amsterdams Peil (Normal Amsterdam Level), a fixed point against which measurements of sea level are made. The NAP is the standard for altitude measurements in Europe. The first two columns show the current sea level at Vlissingen (a city at the mouth of the Scheldt estuary in the southwestern part of the country) and Ijmuiden (a town at the mouth of the North Sea Canal);

the third, 4.55m (15 ft.) above your head, shows the high-water mark during the disastrous floods in Zeeland in 1953. 🕐 *1 hr. Come Mon–Fri to avoid the worst of the crowds. Market open daily 10am–5pm. Waterlooplein.*

❷ ★★★ Museum Het Rembrandthuis. Continue down on Waterlooplein to the end and turn left on Jodenbreestraat. Here you'll find Rembrandt's house, now a fabulously preserved museum. Although Rembrandt was not Jewish, he often painted portraits of his Jewish friends and neighbors. A visit to the museum will not only give you an insight into the artist's life and work but will also give you an opportunity to see the interior and furnishings of a 17th-century home in this area. The house was constructed in 1606; Rembrandt bought it in 1639 and lived here until he went bankrupt in 1658. 🕐 *1 hr. Arrive here an hour or*

Waterlooplein Flea Market.

The interior of Rembrandt House.

2 before closing to avoid the crowds. Visit on Wed or weekends if you're interested in etching demonstrations. Jodenbreestraat 4–6 (at Waterlooplein). ☎ *020/520-0400. www.rembrandthuis.nl. Admission 7€. Mon–Sat 10am–5pm; Sun & holidays 1–5pm. Closed Jan 1. Tram: 9 or 14 to Waterlooplein. For more information, see p 19, bullet* ❼*.*

③ Puccini. Just across the bridge to Staalstraat (keep the water to your right when leaving the Rembrandt House), you'll find this delightful bakery and cafe that makes luscious pastries, tarts, and sandwiches. Try one of the fresh berry pies if it's summer, or a pear or apple pie if it's winter. *Staalstraat 17.* ☎ *020/427-8341. $.*

④ Jewish Resistance Fighters Memorial. Retrace your steps across the bridge and turn right to see this striking black marble monument. It's dedicated to those Jews who tried to resist or escape Nazi oppression and to the people who helped them.

⑤ Blauwbrug (Blue Bridge). Turn left at the monument (the Amstel River will be to your right) and walk toward this notable bridge with its blue lanterns. The cast-iron bridge, inspired by Paris's Pont Alexandre III and opened in 1884, is named after a 16th-century timber bridge painted blue after the 1578 Protestant takeover. Amsterdam's great Impressionist artist George Hendrik Breitner (1857–1923) painted a picture of this bridge in the 1880s.

⑥ Special Moments. Don't cross the Blauwbrug; instead, continue straight ahead, keeping the river to your right. Go left on Nieuwe Herengracht. At no. 33 you'll see the building that was once a Portuguese Jewish home for seniors (they had room for only 10 people and they had their own synagogue inside). Walk to the end of the street and turn right across Vaz Diasbrug. Take a look back down the canal as you cross the bridge and you'll find a picture-perfect view of canal houses and houseboats that's very typically Amsterdam. Continue along this road (Weesperstraat) until you reach a small garden. Here, you'll find a monument to Dutch people who protected their Jewish compatriots during World War II. The memorial, from 1950, takes the shape of a white limestone altar, and has reliefs of mourning men, women, and children. This is a great garden for a moment of contemplation.

⑦ ★★★ Joods Historisch Museum (Jewish Historical Museum). Head back up Weesperstraat and turn left to reach this museum. This building once housed four synagogues built by Jewish refugees from Germany and Poland in the 17th and 18th centuries. The buildings survived the Nazi occupation of Amsterdam during World

War II more or less intact. They were sold to the city in 1955 and stood empty for many years. In 1987 they became home to an impressive collection of paintings and decorative and ceremonial objects that were looted during the war. In addition to admiring the beauty of the buildings themselves (which include the oldest public synagogue in Europe), you can enjoy some short documentaries about Jewish customs and traditions such as bar mitzvahs and funerals. The museum regularly holds special screenings of features and award-winning documentaries pertaining to Jewish history and culture. ⏱ *1½ hr. Jonas Daniel Meijerplein 2–4.* ☎ *020/626-9945. www.jhm.nl. Admission 6.50€. Daily 11am–5pm. Tram: 9 or 14 to Waterlooplein.*

❽ The Dockworker. Jonas Daniël Meijerplein is where many Jews were forced to wait for their deportation to concentration camps. This bronze statue by Mari Andriessen was erected in 1952 in

A menorah at the Jewish Historical Museum.

commemoration of the 1941 February Strike by the workers of Amsterdam to protest the deportation of the city's Jewish population. The strike, one of the biggest collective actions in all of occupied Europe against the Nazi persecution, was ruthlessly suppressed.

❾ Wertheim Park. This small park—really it's more like a large garden—is a good place for a rest, on benches around its rim. At the park's center is a memorial by sculptor Jan Wolkers to the victims of Auschwitz. Six large "broken" mirrors laid flat on the ground reflect a shattered sky and cover a buried urn containing ashes of the dead from the concentration camp. NOOIT MEER AUSCHWITZ (NEVER AGAIN AUSCHWITZ) reads the dedication. An information board lists in impersonal round numbers some of the gruesome statistics of the Holocaust: Of 140,000 members of Holland's Jewish community, 107,000 were deported to concentration camps, and just 5,200 returned; of the 95,000 sent to Auschwitz and Sobibor, fewer than 500 survived. One of those who perished (at Bergen-Belsen) was Anne Frank, who has a street named after her at the far end of the park.

The Old Center

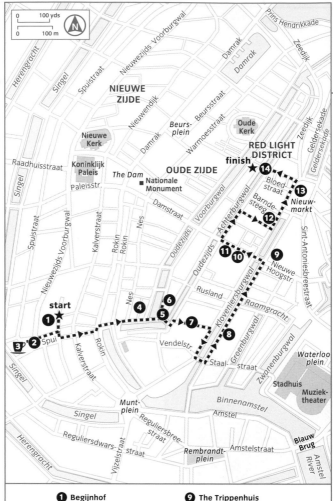

0 ____ 100 yds
0 ____ 100 m

Prins Hendrikkade

Herengracht

Singel

Spuistraat

Nieuwezijds Voorburgwal

Nieuwendijk

Damrak

Damrak

Damrok

Zeedijk

NIEUWE ZIJDE

Beursstraat

Beursplein

Warmoesstraat

Oude Kerk

RED LIGHT DISTRICT

finish ★ 14

Nieuwe Kerk

Raadhuisstraat

Koninklijk Paleis

Paleisstr.

The Dam

Nationale Monument

OUDE ZIJDE

Damstraat

Voorburgwal

Oudezijds

Bloedstraat

13

Barnde-steeg

Nieuw-markt

12

Zeedijk

Geldersekade

Geldersekade

Singel

Spuistraat

Nieuwezijds Voorburgwal

Kalverstraat

Rokin

Rokin

Nes

Nes

Achterburgwal

Oudezijds

11 10

9

Nieuwe Hoogstr.

Sint-Antoniesbreestraat

start
★
1

3 2

Spui

Kalverstraat

Rokin

4

6

5

7

Rusland

Raamgracht

Kloveniersburgwal

Groenburgwal

8

Zwanenburgwal

Waterlooplein

Vendelstr.

Staal- straat

Stadhuis

Muziektheater

Muntplein

Singel

Herengracht

Reguliersdwars-straat

Vijzelstraat

Reguliersbree-straat

Binnenamstel

Amstel

Amstelstraat

Rembrandt-plein

Blauw Brug

Amstel River

1 Begijnhof
2 Spui
3 Café Luxembourg
4 Gebed Zonder End
5 Huis aan de Drie Grachten
6 Agnietenkapel
7 Oudemanhuispoort
8 The Poppenhuis

9 The Trippenhuis
10 Oost Indisch Huis
11 Narrowest Houses
12 Amsterdams Brouwhuis Maximiliaan
13 De Waag
14 Red Light District & China Town

This walk takes you into the heart of the oldest part of the city, where you can see the oldest remaining structure in Amsterdam as well as the city's narrowest houses. This is the core of Amsterdam, the epicenter from which the city expanded into other directions. Take this walk in the afternoon if you can, and leave yourself some time to people-watch at one of the city's infamous cafes. The walk ends near the Red Light District. START: **Begijnhof (tram 1, 2, or 5 to Spui).**

1 ★★★ **Begijnhof.** This cluster of small homes around a lovely garden courtyard is the best place to appreciate the history of old Amsterdam. No. 34 is the city's oldest house, built in 1425 as a home for devout women. It is one of only two timber houses remaining in the city. Amsterdam was a destination for religious pilgrims and an important Catholic center. The Begijnhof (a cloister) offered women the option to live without a husband and children, and without becoming a nun, at a time when there was little in the way of alternatives. Originally it was surrounded by water, with access via a bridge over the Begijnesloot canal. It remained in operation even after the 1578 changeover of the city from Catholicism to Protestantism. The last *begijn*

The Begijnhof garden.

closed in 1971, but you can still pay homage to these pious women by pausing for a moment at the small flower-planed mound that lies just at the center garden's edge, across from the Engelse Kerk (English Church), which dates back to 1607. Opposite the front of the church, at no. 30, is the Begijnhofkapel, a secret Catholic chapel from 1671 that's still in use today. The houses are now a home for seniors. ⏱ *30 min. From Spui, take the alleyway Gedempte Begijnensloot to the cloister. No phone. Free admission. Daily 8am–1pm. Tram: 1, 2, or 5 to Spui. Map p 60.*

2 **Spui.** This square is both elegant and animated. At its south end is a statue of a small boy, *Het Lieverje* (The Little Darling), who is supposed

Spui square.

to represent a typical Amsterdam child. Across the street, at no. 21, is the Maagdenhuis, the main downtown building of the University of Amsterdam.

3 ★★ **Café Luxembourg.** The *New York Times* named this bohemian place "one of the world's greatest cafes." Though I wouldn't go that far, it's certainly one of the world's top 50 cafes. The delightful sidewalk tables are a wonderful place to people-watch in summer while enjoying a toasted Gouda sandwich and a cup of strong Dutch coffee, served with syrupy-sweet condensed milk. *Spuistraat 22–24.* ☎ *020/620-6264. $$.*

4 **Gebed Zonder End (Prayer Without End).** This alleyway is located in the district known as De Wallen (The Walls); its name comes from the convents that used to be here. Legend has it that you could always hear the murmur of prayers from behind the walls. You are in the heart of Old Amsterdam here— the streets are narrow and a bit

confusing. *To reach the alleyway, go to the end of Spui & cross Rokin & Nes sts., walking along Lange Brugsteeg to Grimburgwal.*

5 **Huis aan de Drie Grachten (House on the Three Canals).** Continue on Grimburgwal and cross Oudezijds Voorburgwal and Oudezijds Achterburgwal. Between these two canals you'll find this handsome red-brick, step-gabled, Dutch Renaissance house from 1609. It has red-painted wooden shutters and is constantly being restored. It used to be an antiquarian bookstore. *Oudezijds Voorburgwal 249.*

6 **Agnietenkapel.** Stroll a short way along Oudezijds Voorburgwal canal to no. 231, where you'll spot an elaborately ornamental gateway from 1571. This was the chapel of the St. Agnes Convent until the Protestant takeover of Amsterdam. It later formed part of the Athenaeum Illustre, the city's first university, and now houses the university museum, which is not very interesting unless there's a special exhibit. *231 Oudezijds Voorburgwal.*

Detail of the portal at Agnietenkapel.

De Waag.

7 Oudemanhuispoort. Backtrack to the House on the Three Canals and cross the bridge to the far side of Oudezijds Achterburgwal. You'll pass the Gasthuis, once a hospital and now part of the University of Amsterdam campus, and turn right onto a dimly lit arcade, the Oudemanhuispoort, that hosts a secondhand-book market Monday to Saturday 10:30am to 6pm. If you're interested, browse around here for a few minutes. In the middle of the arcade, on the left, you'll see a doorway leading to a courtyard garden with a statue of Minerva. It's a lovely place for a few quiet minutes of peace.

8 The Poppenhuis. Turn right on Kloveniersburgwal and cross over the canal and go left to reach this lovely classical mansion built in 1642 for Joan Poppen, a dissolute grandson and heir to a rich German merchant. The youth hostel next door at no. 97 was originally a home for retired sea captains. *95 Kloveniersburgwal.*

9 The Trippenhuis. Nearby you'll see this house built between 1660 and 1664 for the Trip brothers, who were arms dealers (which explains the martial images and emblems dotted about the house). Originally there were two houses behind a single classical facade, but the two have since been joined. It now houses the Royal Netherlands Academy of Science and is not open for visitors. *29 Kloveniersburgwal.*

10 Oost Indisch Huis (East India House). Backtrack to the canal bridge and cross over to Oude Hoogstraat, where you can enter this 1606 building via a courtyard on the left side of the street. Once the headquarters of the United East India Company, the house now belongs to the University of Amsterdam. It's not officially open for visits, but you can stroll into the courtyard and through the doors to take a peek at the hallways hung with paintings of the 17th-century Dutch trading settlement of Batavia (now Jakarta, Indonesia). *Oude Hoogstraat.*

11 Narrowest Houses. Nearby you'll spot one of the city's narrowest houses at no. 22 Oude Hoogstraat. Backtrack to Kloveniersburgwal and go left. At no. 26 you'll see the Klein

Shopping at De Bijenkorf

After all this history you may be eager to return to the modern age—and what better way than through some rampant consumerism? De Bijenkorf is Amsterdam's best department store, selling a terrific variety of goods. If you forgot something at home, you can probably find a replacement here. See p 72.

Trippenhuis, the narrow house of the Trip brothers' coachman (see p 28, bullet ③). A few doors down, at nos. 10–12, is the drugstore Jacob Hooy & Co., which has been dispensing medicinal relief since 1743.

⑫ Amsterdams Brouwhuis Maximiliaan. This is the city's smallest brewery, in a surviving part of the 16th-century Bethanien Convent. It produces 10 different beers and serves them from copper vats. The nuns who once brewed their own beer here have long since departed, but their beer-making tradition continues in this brewery, which has a rustic but chic wood-floored bar and restaurant attached. There are beers to suit all tastes here, from ale to red to dark. The menu includes many dishes with beer as an ingredient, but I wouldn't particularly recommend a meal here. *6–8 Kloveniersburgwal.*

⑬ De Waag (Weight House). Kloveniersburgwal ends at the large Nieuwmarkt square, where you'll easily spot the massive edifice that was once the city's medieval gates, and later the Weight House and guild offices. *See p 28, bullet ①.*

⑭ Red Light District & China Town. Nieuwmarkt is the gateway to both the city's Chinatown and Red Light District. Small, family-run Chinese restaurants abound on the square and the little streets leading away from it. This is also a good chance to tour the Red Light District (see p 14, bullet ⑧). To do that, take Monnickenstraat to Oudezijds Achterburgwal and turn right, and you'll find many windows that frame prostitutes waiting for customers. When you're finished strolling, you can catch the Nieuwmarkt metro or walk the 10 minutes to Centraal Station or the Dam to catch a tram.●

Shopping Best Bets

Best **Wine Shop**
★ De Ware Jacob, *Herenstraat 41* (p 76)

Best for **Antique Maps**
★ A. van der Meer, *P.C. Hoofstraat* (p 70)

Best **Delftware**
★ Heinen, *Prinsengracht 440* (p 72)

Best **English-Language Bookstore**
★ American Book Center, *Kalverstraat 185* (p 71); and Evenaar, *Singel 348* (p 71)

Best **Place to Score Castro's Favorite Stogies**
P.G.C. Hajenius, *Rokin 92–96* (p 72)

Best **Place to Shop for Diamonds**
★ Gassan Diamonds, *Nieuwe Uilenburgerstraat 173–175* (p 74)

Best **Place to Pick Up Authentic Hunks of Gouda**
★ De Kaaskamer, *Runstraat 7* (p 71)

Best **Dutch Designer Shoes**
★★ Jan Jansen, *Roelof Hartstraat 16* (p 76)

Best **Street Market**
★★ Albert Cuyp Markt, *Albert Cuypstraat* (p 75)

Best **Places to Provision for Romance**
E Kramer Candle Shop, *Reestraat 20* (p 71); and ★ Bloomings, *Prinsenstraat 19* (p 74)

Best Place to **Stop and Smell the Flowers**
★ Bloemenmarkt (Flower Market), *along the Singel by Muntplein* (p 75)

Best Place to **Shop for Picnic Provisions**
★ Boerenmarkt (Farmers Market), *Noordermarkt* (p 76)

Best Places to **Shop for Gifts for Friends Back Home**
Victoria Gifts, *Prins Hendrikkade 47* (p 72); and Lush, *Kalverstraat 98* (p 75)

Best **Department Store**
★★ Metz & Co, *Keizersgracht 455* (p 73)

Best for **Antique Clocks**
★ Marcel Toebosch, *Nieuwe Spiegelstraat 33–35* (p 72)

Best **Designer Boutique for Men, Women & Teens**
★★ Azzurro Due, *P.C. Hoofstraat 122* (p 73)

Best for **Unusual Kids' Toys**
Bell Tree, *Spiegelgracht 10* (p 75)

Best **Designer Goods at Discount Prices**
★★ Megazino, *Rozengracht 207–214* (p 73)

Best **Designer Clothing for Kids**
Oilily, *P.C. Hoofstraat 131–133* (p 75)

Albert Cuyp Markt and Bloemenmarkt are both good places to pick up some fresh blooms.

Museumplein Area **Shopping**

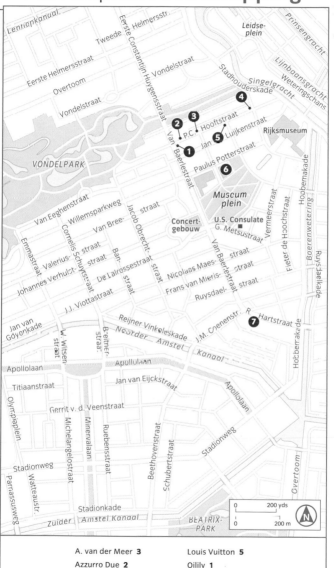

A. van der Meer **3**	Louis Vuitton **5**
Azzurro Due **2**	Oilily **1**
Cartier **4**	van Gogh Museum
Jan Jansen **7**	Gift Shop **6**

Central Amsterdam **Shopping**

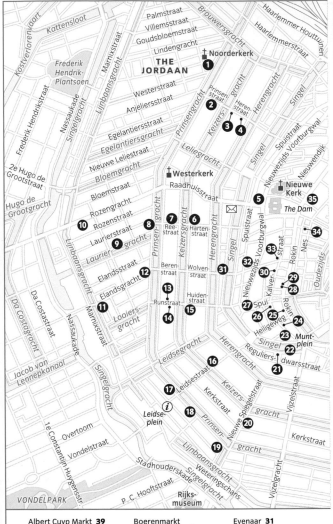

Albert Cuyp Markt **39**	Boerenmarkt	Evenaar **31**
American Book Center **24**	(Farmer's Market) **1**	Gassan Diamonds **37**
Analik **6**	De Bijenkorf **35**	Gerda's Bloemen
Bell Tree **19**	De Kaaskamer **14**	& Planten **13**
Betsy Palmer **34**	De Praktijk **9**	Gort **4**
Bloemenmarkt	De Ware Jacob **3**	Heinen **17**
(Flower Market) **22**	E Kramer	HEMA **23**
Bloomings **2**	Candle Shop **7**	Intermale **32**

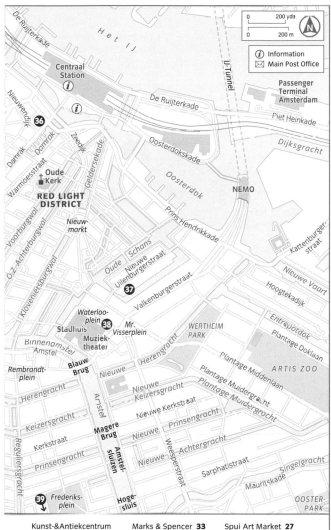

Kunst-&Antiekcentrum
De Looier (Antiques) **11**
La Savonnerie **12**
Lush **30**
Magic Mushroom
Gallery **21**
Magna Plaza **5**
Marcel Toebosch **20**

Marks & Spencer **33**
Mathieu Hart **25**
Megazino **10**
Metz & Co **16**
P.G.C. HaJenlus **29**
Premsela &
Hamburger **28**
Smokiana **18**

Spui Art Market **27**
't Winkeltje **8**
van Ravenstein **15**
Victoria Gifts **36**
Waterlooplein
Flea Market **38**
Waterstone's
Booksellers **26**

Amsterdam Shopping A to Z

Antiques

★ **A. van der Meer** MUSE-UMPLEIN   Smack in the midst of the fashionable stores on P.C. Hoofstraat, this peaceful shop has an extensive collection of 17th- and 18th-century Dutch world maps by the early cartographers Blaeu, Hondius, and Marcator, among other maps, prints, and engravings. *P.C. Hoofstraat 112.* ☎ *020/662-1936. AE, MC, V. Tram: 1, 2, or 5 to Hobbema-straat. Map p 67.*

Premsela & Ham-burger OLD CENTER Opened in 1823, this fine jewelry and antique sil-ver seller—purveyors to the Dutch court—boasts a great collection of Old Dutch Silver by 17th-century craftsmen. Their work-shop designs and repairs jewelry. *Rokin 98.* ☎ *020/624-9688. AE, MC, V. Tram: 4, 9, 14, 16, 24, or 25 to Spui. Map p 68.*

An antique Dutch silver teapot.

Art

★ **De Praktijk** JORDAAN   Run by a local dentist-turned-art-dealer, this Jordaan gallery focuses on moder-ately priced modern Dutch painting and photography. Open Wednesday to Saturday only. *Lauriergracht 96.* ☎ *020/422-1727. MC, V. Tram: 6, 13, 14, or 17 to Marnix-straat. Map p 68.*

Mathieu Hart OLD CENTER   Since 1878 this refined store has been selling color etch-ings of Dutch cities, along with rare old prints, 18th-century delftware, and grand-father clocks. *Rokin 122.* ☎ *020/623-1658. AE, MC, V. Tram: 1, 4, 9, 14, 16, 24, or 25 to Spui. Map p 68.*

★ **van Gogh Museum Gift Shop** MUSEUMPLEIN   One of the best museum gift stores in the city sells everything from imitations of van Gogh's classics to beautiful

If you can't afford the real thing, shop for prints, reproductions, art books, and more at the van Gogh Museum Gift Shop.

You may have a hard time choosing from the hundreds of cheeses for sale at De Kaaskamer.

mugs painted with his famous sunflowers, plus a good selection of art books. *Paulus Potterstraat 7.* ☎ *020/570-5200. www.vangogh museum.nl. AE, MC, V. Tram: 1, 2, or 5 to Museumplein. Map p 67.*

Books

★ **American Book Center** OLD CENTER From novels and Frommer's guides to the latest magazines, this large U.S.-style bookstore is extremely well stocked. *Kalverstraat 185.* ☎ *020/625-5537 AE, DC, MC, V. Tram: 4, 9, 14, 16, 24, or 25 to Muntplein. Map p 68.*

Evenaar CANAL BELT Specializing in travel literature, this very well-situated bookstore has everything from travel guides and world maps to all sorts of books on armchair travel and anthropology. You can also find antique travel books here. *Singel 348.* ☎ *020/624-6289. AE, MC, V. Tram: 1, 2, or 5 to Spui. Map p 68.*

Intermale OLD CENTER This large bookstore claims to have the largest collection of books of interest to gay men in Europe. In addition to books, magazines, and greeting cards in English, they stock Dutch and German periodicals. *Spuistraat*

251. ☎ *020/625-0009. MC, V. Tram: 1, 2, or 5 to Spui. Map p 68.*

Waterstone's Booksellers OLD CENTER This British chain is very well stocked with the latest fiction and nonfiction releases. You'll find lots of hardcovers here, but they have a wide selection of paperbacks as well. *Kalverstraat 152.* ☎ *020/ 638-3821. www.waterstones.co.uk. AE, DC, MC, V. Tram: 1, 2, 4, 5, 14, 16, 17, 24, or 25 to Spui. Map p 68.*

Candles

E Kramer Candle Shop CANAL BELT All kinds of candles are sold here, from elaborately carved melting works of art to outrageously kitschy wax designs. A good place to pick up scented candles and votives if you're planning a romantic evening in your hotel room. *Reestraat 20.* ☎ *020/ 626-5274. MC, V. Tram: 6, 13, 14, or 17 to Westermarkt. Map p 68.*

Cheese

★ **De Kaaskamer** OLD CENTER Choose from over 300 cheeses at this shop (they will vacuum-pack for travelers) including rows and rows of authentic wheels of Gouda stamped with their farm of origin. *Runstraat 7.* ☎ *020/623-3483. MC, V. Tram: 1, 2, or 5 to Spui. Map p 68.*

Most people associate smoking in Amsterdam with marijuana, but cigar-lovers can pick up some fine Cubans here.

reasonable prices. *Prins Hendrikkade 47.* ☎ *020/427-2051. MC, V. Tram: 1, 2, 4, 5, 6, 9, 13, 16, 17, 24, or 25 to Centraal Station. Map p 68.*

Delftware

★ **Heinen** CANAL BELT   A father-and-son team hand-paint the pottery here; you can even watch them in action. They are also official dealers of De Porcelyne Fles and Tichelaars delftware. *Prinsengracht 440.* ☎ *020/421-8360. MC, V. Tram: 6, 7, or 10 to Spiegelgracht. Map p 68.*

Cigars

P.G.C. Hajenius OLD CENTER   This store has been around since 1826, and it's the best place to shop for Cuban cigars—there's an entire room stocked with Havanas. You'll also find Dutch handmade clay pipes that make good gifts. *Rokin 92–96.* ☎ *020/623-7494. www.hajenius.com. AE, DC, MC, V. Tram: 1, 2, 4, 5, 14, 16, 24, or 25 to Spui. Map p 68.*

A hand-painted Delft tile makes a great gift for friends back home.

Smokiana CANAL BELT   In addition to cigars, Smokiana sells just about every kind of pipe imaginable, from the antique to the exotic to the downright weird. *Prinsengracht 488.* ☎ *020/421-1779. MC, V. Tram: 1, 2, or 5 to Prinsengracht. Map p 68.*

Clocks

★ **Marcel Toebosch** OLD CENTER   One of the most impressive collections of antique clocks can be found in this exquisite store, along with music boxes and Louis 14th chandeliers. *Nieuwe Spiegelstraat 33–35.* ☎ *020/625-2732. AE, DC, MC, V. Tram: 1, 2, or 5 to Koningsplein. Map p 68.*

Victoria Gifts OLD CENTER   This small store is great for finding Dutch clocks and other quality gifts at

Department Stores

De Bijenkorf OLD CENTER   The city's best-known department store sports the largest variety of goods. From handbags to big-screen TVs, it's all here. *Dam 1.* ☎ *020/621-8080. AE, DC, MC, V. Tram: 4, 9, 14, 16, 24, or 25 to the Dam. Map p 68.*

HEMA OLD CENTER   This smaller store is a great place to find a cheap item (gloves, hat, socks) or just a toothbrush. You can get mineral water in large bottles here, too.

Magna Plaza's elegant interior.

Kalvertoren Shopping Center, Kalverstraat 212. ☎ 020/626-8720. MC, V.
Tram: 4, 9, 14, 16, 24, or 25 to Muntplein. Map p 68.

★★ Magna Plaza OLD CENTER
This is more like an elegant
mall than a depart-
ment store,
with four
floors filled
with about
50 specialist stores
from The Body Shop
to the Gourmet
Cheese Shop.
*Nieuwezijds Voor-
burgwal 182. ☎ 020/626-9199. www.
magnaplaza.nl. AE, DC, MC, V. Tram:
4, 9, 14, 16, 24, or 25 to the Dam.
Map p 68.*

*Shop for all sorts of designer goods at
Amsterdam's Louis Vuitton boutique.*

Marks & Spencer OLD CENTER
A branch of the popular British chain
store very similar to those in London.
Everything from underwear to a food
hall with fresh ready-made food,
good for simple picnics or to take
back to your hotel room. *Kalverstraat
66–72. ☎ 020/531-2468. AE, DC, MC,
V. Tram: 4, 9, 14, 16, 24, or 25 to the
Dam. Map p 68.*

★★ Metz & Co CANAL BELT
Founded in 1740, this is Amsterdam's
most upscale department store (like a
small Harrods), selling everything
from beautiful furniture to gourmet
kitchenware. Don't miss the rooftop
cafe with its fantastic view of the city.
*Keizersgracht 455. ☎ 020/520-7020.
AE, DC, MC, V. Tram: 1, 2, or 5 to
Keizersgracht. Map p 68.*

Fashion
★ Analik OLD CENTER   This two-
room store is named after one of
Amsterdam's renowned designers.
One room is filled with small pieces
of clothing for young and skinny
women, the other with funky handbags and other accessories designed
by local Dutch artists. *Hartenstraat

34–36. ☎ 020/422-0561. AE, MC, V.
Tram: 1, 2, or 5 to Spui. Map p 68.*

★★ kids Azzurro Due MUSE-
UMPLEIN   The ultimate
address for finding a pair of
designer jeans or that elu-
sive Prada accessory for
both men and women.
Azzurro kids is two
doors down at no. 122.
Very chic, very trendy.
*P.C. Hoofstraat 122. ☎ 020/
671-6804. AE, DC,
MC, V. Tram: 1, 2,
or 5 to Hobbema-
straat. Map p 67.*

★ Louis Vuitton MUSEUMPLEIN
Of course, you'll find the usual upmarket suitcases and handbags here that
Vuitton is famous for, but you'll also
find a good selection of shoes, jewelry, belts, and ties. *P.C. Hoofstraat
65–67. ☎ 020/575-5775. AE, DC, MC,
V. Tram: 1, 2, or 5 to Hobbemastraat.
Map p 67.*

★★ Megazino JORDAAN   This
huge designer outlet store sells
everything from Armani, Gucci, and
Prada to Calvin Klein and Dolce &

Metz & Co.

Gabbana—all at 30% to 50% off the original price. A great place to burn some plastic without breaking the bank. *Rozengracht 207–214.* ☎ *020/330-1031. AE, MC, V. Tram: 6, 13, 14, or 17 to Westermarkt. Map p 68.*

★ **van Ravenstein** CANAL BELT This small fashion boutique carries the latest creations by up-and-coming Dutch and Belgian designers such as Victor and Rolf, Martin Margiela, Dirk Bikkembergs, and Bernhard Willhelm. In the basement, there's a collection of last season's discards on sale. *Keizersgracht 359.* ☎ *020/639-0067. AE, MC, V. Tram: 13, 14, or 17. Map p 68.*

Flowers

★ **Bloomings** JORDAAN This friendly neighborhood florist sells expertly arranged flowers and exquisite vases of all shapes and sizes. *Prinsenstraat 19.* ☎ *020/622-3585. MC, V. Tram: 6, 13, 14, or 17 to Westermarkt. Map p 68.*

Gerda's Bloemen & Planten OLD CENTER One of the most elegant florists in the city boasts a fantastic selection of exotic flowers and unusual plants artfully arranged and presented. *Runstraat 16.* ☎ *020/624-2912. MC, V. Tram: 1, 2, or 5 to Spui. Map p 68.*

Funky Shops
Magic Mushroom Gallery OLD CENTER Only in Amsterdam. Everything from "psychoactive mushrooms" to tonics such as Yohimbe Rush and Horn E that allegedly improve your sex life. *Singel 524.* ☎ *020/422-7845. MC, V. Tram: 4, 9, 14, 16, 24, or 25 to Muntplein. Map p 68.*

kids 't Winkeltje JORDAAN This funky but fun store sells modern versions of old tin cars, colored bottles and glasses, lamps shaped like bananas, and some children's toys

from the 1950s. *Prinsengracht 228.* ☎ *020/625-1352. MC, V. Tram: 6, 13, 14, or 17 to Westermarkt. Map p 68.*

Jewelry
★★ **Cartier** MUSEUMPLEIN If you must have the best, you've come to the right place. You'll find intricately designed jewelry, watches, pens, and other accessories at this quintessential French shop found the world over on the swankiest city blocks. *P.C. Hoofstraat 30.* ☎ *020/670-3434. www.cartier.com. AE, DC, MC, V. Tram: 1, 2, or 5 to Hobbemastraat. Map p 67.*

★ **Gassan Diamonds** OLD CENTER This undisputed leader of the city's diamond trade is housed in a stunning Amsterdam School–style building. In addition to shopping for diamonds, you can take a tour that shows you how the jewels are cut. *Nieuwe Uilenburgerstraat 173–175.* ☎ *020/622-5333. AE, DC, MC, V. www.gassandiamonds.com. Tram: 9, 14, or 20 to Waterlooplein. Map p 68.*

★ **Gort** JORDAAN This beautiful little shop specializes in unique and innovative jewelry design. If you like modern and minimalist designs, then

Fresh tulips for sale at one of Amsterdam's many florists.

this place is for you. *Herenstraat 11.* ☎ *020/620-6240. MC, V. Tram: 6, 13, 14, or 17 to Westermarkt. Map p 68.*

Kids
kids Bell Tree CANAL BELT This unique store sells modern versions of old wood toys. Very Dutch. A great place to find an unusual gift for a child. *Spiegelgracht 10–12.* ☎ *020/625-8830. MC, V. Tram: 6, 7, or 10 to Spiegelgracht. Map p 68.*

Oilily MUSEUMPLEIN Amsterdam's most upscale children's clothing store has been on the fashion scene since 1963 (they now sell some women's clothing, too). They are known for extremely colorful designs of very high quality. *PC Hoofstraat 131–133.* ☎ *020/672-3361. AE, DC, MC, V. Tram: 2 or 5 to Hobbemastraat. Map p 67.*

Shoes
★ Betsy Palmer OLD CENTER Imelda Marcos would not approve. There are no classic shoes here, but there's an incredible collection of trendy women's footwear, with obscure but fun brands like Sexy Chic, Sunloving Babe, and Serious Partying. *Rokin 9–15.* ☎ *020/422-1040. www.betsypalmer.com. AE, DC, MC, V. Tram: 4, 9, 14, 16, 24, or 25 to the Dam. Map p 68.*

★★ Jan Jansen MUSEUMPLEIN Award-winning Dutch shoe designer Jan Jansen sells his men's and women's footwear in this chic store. You can special-order colors and sizes if you can't find yours—it takes about 3 weeks and they will mail your shoes to you. *Roelof Hartstraat 16.* ☎ *020/470-0116. www.janjansenshoes.com. AE, DC, MC, V. Tram: 1, 2, or 5 to Roelof Hartstraat. Map p 67.*

Soap
★ kids La Savonnerie JORDAAN Artisanal soaps of all shapes and

Gassan Diamonds offers an informative tour in addition to dazzling gems.

sizes are on sale here. The soap chess set makes a great gift. You can buy personalized soap and even make your own. Kids enjoy the animal-shaped soaps. *Prinsengracht 294.* ☎ *020/428-1139. MC, V. Tram: 7, 10, or 17 to Elandsgracht. Map p 68.*

Lush OLD CENTER This very popular British chain store sells fragrant and fresh handmade soaps in all flavors and sizes. It's a fun place even for just a quick browse (and a sniff), and their attractive gift-packaging makes for great souvenir shopping. *Kalverstraat 98.* ☎ *020/330-6376. www.lush.co.uk. AE, MC, V. Tram: 4, 9, 14, 16, 24, or 25 to the Dam. Map p 68.*

Street Markets
★★ Albert Cuyp Markt PIJP Unofficially referred to as Europe's largest market, this is Amsterdam's liveliest and most-frequented all-purpose street market, stretching for about 1km (½ mile). From fresh herring and Gouda to silk scarves and hand-knitted hats, you'll find it here Monday to Saturday 9am to 6pm. *Albert Cuypstraat. No phone. No credit cards. Tram: 16, 24, or 25 to Albert Cuypstraat. Map p 68.*

★ Bloemenmarkt (Flower Market) CANAL BELT Floating on

a row of permanently moored barges, this is Amsterdam's most popular flower market. You'll find everything from fresh-cut flowers and bright plants to rows and rows of tulip bunches. Fresh-cut tulips cost about the same here as they do at flower stands around town, but this is a great place to pick up ready-to-travel packets of tulip bulbs. Open daily 8am to 8pm. *Along the Singel by Muntplein. No phone. No credit cards. Tram: 9, 14, 16, 24, or 25 to Muntplein. Map p 68.*

★ Boerenmarkt (Farmers Market) JORDAAN

Also known as the Bio (or organic) market, the Boerenmarkt caters to the trendy locals who live in the elegant Jordaan neighborhood. A great place to find fresh vegetables, fruit, cheeses, and organic breads for a picnic. Open Saturday 9am to 5pm. *Noordermarkt. No phone. No credit cards. Tram: 3 or 10 to Noordermarkt. Map p 68.*

Kunst-&Antiekcentrum De Looier (Antiques) JORDAAN

A large indoor antique market spread throughout several old warehouses. You'll find everything from furniture and old armoires to 19th-century tin toys, Delft tiles, Dutch knickknacks, and antique jewelry. Open Saturday

to Thursday 11am to 5pm. *Elands-gracht 109.* ☎ *020/624-9038. No credit cards. Tram: 7, 10, or 17 to Elandsgracht. Map p 68.*

Spui Art Market OLD CENTER

Every Sunday (10am–6pm) from April to November, local artists mount outdoor exhibits here. You may have to wade through a lot of mediocrity, but it's possible to find something special here. *Spui. No phone. No credit cards. Tram: 1, 2, or 5 to Spui. Map p 68.*

Waterlooplein Flea Market

CANAL BELT This classic Amsterdam street market has everything from bargain-basement souvenirs to antiques, old CDs, leather jackets, and woolen hats. The market is open Monday to Saturday from 10am to 5pm. *Waterlooplein. No phone. No credit cards. Tram: 9 or 14 to Waterlooplein. Map p 68.*

Wine

★ De Ware Jacob JORDAAN

Since 1970 this small but charming wine shop has carried the finest wines from boutique wineries around the world. *Herenstraat 41.* ☎ *020/623-9877. MC, V. Tram: 6, 13, 14, or 17 to Westermarkt. Map p 68.* ●

A food stand at Albert Cuyp Markt.

5 The Best of the **Outdoors**

Strolling in **Vondelpark**

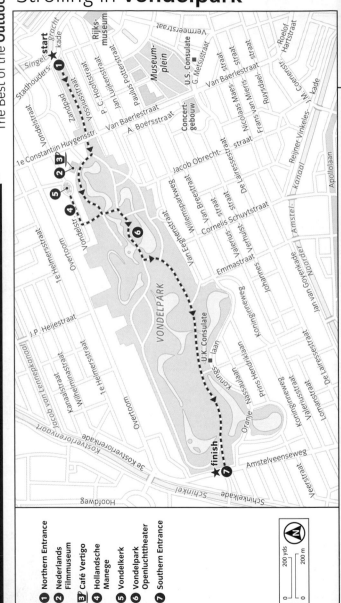

1. Northern Entrance
2. Nederlands Filmmuseum
3. Café Vertigo
4. Hollandsche Manege
5. Vondelkerk
6. Vondelpark Openluchttheater
7. Southern Entrance

200 yds

200 m

Amsterdam is not a green city, but Vondelpark provides a tranquil refuge from the bustling crowds. Trees, English-style manicured rose gardens, ponds, and trails for bikers and in-line skaters abound. Many commuters just use the park to cross from the city's southern neighborhoods to its center. Always watch out for speeding bikes as you walk through the park. START: **Tram 2 or 5 to Hobbemastraat.**

❶ ★★ Northern Entrance.
Enter the park through the gates closest to the Rijksmuseum, on the corner of Vossiusstraat and Stadhouderskade. This entrance is just a 5-minute walk from Leidseplein. A sculpture of the *Maid of Amsterdam,* a symbol of the city, sits over these gates. Keep to your right to avoid the multitudes of zooming bikes (motorized vehicles are not allowed in the park). The park was opened to the public in 1865. JD and LP Zocher (a father-and-son operation) landscaped what was then a much smaller space, using ponds and pathways to create an English-style garden. Over the years, some 120 different kinds of trees were planted as the park grew to its present size of roughly 44 hectares (110 acres). *Tram: 2 or 5 to Hobbemastraat.*

❷ ★★ Nederlands Filmmuseum. From the gates, head south, keeping to the path on your right. After about a 10-minute stroll, you'll see this grand pavilion to your right, designed by PJ Hamer (1812–87) and his son, W. Hamer (1843–1913). It was opened in 1881 as a cafe and restaurant, then restored as an international cultural center in 1947. Renovated again in 1991, it is now the country's main film museum. The interior of Amsterdam's first cinema (the Cinema Parisien) was transported here during the last renovations and placed entirely into one of the two theaters. The Art Deco interior alone is worth the price of admission to one of the many screenings that take place here every week. Some films do sell out, so it's not a bad idea to pick up tickets in advance. The two theaters show up to 1,000 films per year, including some English-language films or foreign films with English subtitles. In summer there are occasional free outdoor screenings. *Vondelpark 3. ☎ 020/589-1400. www.filmmuseum.nl. Admission 2€ exhibitions; films 7.20€ Mon–Thurs, 7.80€ Fri–Sun. Museum & library open Tues–Fri 10am–5pm, Sat 11am–5pm; box office Mon–Fri 10am–10pm, Sat 6–10pm; Sun 2–10pm. Screenings daily at 7pm & additionally at 3pm on Sun.*

Nederlands Filmmuseum.

Bicyclists and pedestrians share Vondelpark's paths.

3 ★★ Café Vertigo. This fabulous cafe has an outdoor patio in the midst of Vondelpark. It's connected to the Film Museum and serves the usual coffee, sandwiches, and light meals, but there's also an international menu for lunch and dinner. *Vondelpark 3.* ☎ *020/612-3021. $$.*

4 Hollandsche Manege (Dutch Riding School). When you exit the cafe, stay on the path to the right and you'll see the glorious neoclassical facade of the Dutch Riding School, which was built in 1882. Restored in the 1980s, it still operates as a stable and arena. The building was designed by AL van Gendt (who also designed the Concertgebouw), and was modeled after the Spanish Riding School in Vienna. Go inside for a look at its gilded mirrors and molded horses' heads. Be sure to climb up to the balcony for a panoramic view of the arena. You can see the horses perform every Sunday; shows are usually at 3 and 7pm, but call or e-mail to confirm. You can also sign up for a riding lesson (19€ for an hour); contact the school for details.

Freshening Up Vondelpark

The over 10 million visitors that visit Vondelpark every year are seriously impacting the earth. The park was built on peat and now the ground is a good .6m (2 ft.) lower than the surrounding buildings. When it rains, some areas of the park collect water, resulting in large, unwanted ponds. An ambitious renovation project is in full swing (with most of the funds coming from public donations) to reconnect some of the older ponds and create a new drainage system. The landscapers are also planting new varieties of water-absorbing trees and bushes. The work is done in clusters and only small corners of the park at varying seasons of the year are cordoned off—visitors will hardly notice the renovation.

Rollerblading, Anyone?

When you reach the southern entrance of the park on Amstelveenseweg, you'll find a rental booth with in-line skates. Rates at **Rent A Skate** (☎ 020/664-5091; daily 11am–10pm) are 5€ per hour or 15€ for a full day, for both adults and children, and include protective gear. You'll need to bring along an ID and leave a 20€ refundable deposit. If you're game, try joining the 3,000-odd skaters who strap on their 'blades for the regular **Friday Night Skate.** In the summer months, this event begins at 8pm from the Filmmuseum in Vondelpark and takes a route of 15km (9 miles) through the city.

Vondelstraat 140. ☎ *020/618-0942. info@dehollandschemanege.nl. Free admission. Tues–Fri 10am–6pm; Sat–Sun 2pm–midnight.*

5 **Vondelkerk.** Close to the Riding School, you'll see this large church designed by PJH Cuypers (architect of Centraal Station). It was completed in 1880. A fire in 1904 destroyed its original tower, and a new one was added by the architect's son. In 1985 the church was converted into offices. It's not open to the public, but sometimes cultural events are held here, contact the tourist office for details. *Vondelstraat 120.*

6 ★ **kids** **Vondelpark Open-luchttheater (Vondelpark Open-Air Theater).** Another few minutes' stroll brings you to this open-air venue where summer musical concerts and occasional theater pieces (usually in Dutch) are staged free of charge. For schedule information, contact the VVV (see p 166 for more information). On Wednesday afternoons from May 15 to September 15, children's shows are performed for free. These are usually in Dutch, but emphasis is on mime and sometimes puppets, so children of all nationalities seem to enjoy the show.

7 **Southern Entrance.** By the time you reach the southern gates, you'll have walked a little over 1.5km (1 mile). You can exit here and jump on any tram to Centraal Station, or you can head back north, staying to your right to take the path on the eastern side of the park back to the entrance gates close to the Rijksmuseum. The entire loop measures about 3.8km (2½ miles).

'Blading through Vondelpark is a great way to see the sights and get a little exercise.

Touring Amsterdam by **Canal Bike**

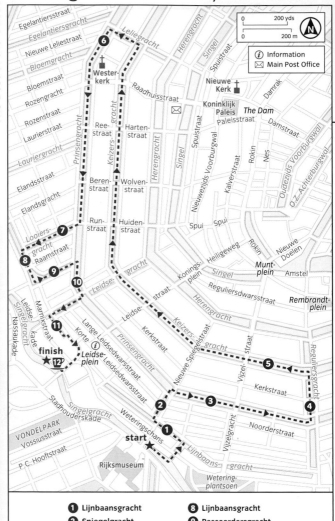

1 Lijnbaansgracht
2 Spiegelgracht
3 Prinsengracht
4 Reguliersgracht
5 Keizersgracht
6 Prinsengracht
7 Looiersgracht

8 Lijnbaansgracht
9 Passeerdersgracht
10 Prinsengracht
   & Leidsegracht
11 Leidsebosje
12 Café Americain

Canal biking down the city's lovely waterways is an outdoor activity unique to Amsterdam. A lot like pedal boats, these "bikes" let you glide quietly down the canals for a close-up look at houseboats and bridges. You'll also get to admire the many 17th- and 18th-century houses that line the canals from a different vantage point. I don't recommend taking kids under 10 on the bikes, but older children will likely remember the experience for the rest of their lives. Early on a summer's evening or late on a winter's afternoon is the best time, when the slanting sun hits the buildings and bridges, affording rich opportunities for photos. START: **Rijksmuseum mooring.**

❶ Lijnbaansgracht. From the Rijksmuseum Mooring, take a left on Lijnbaansgracht canal, with its very low bridge and rows of neck-gabled houses. The name of this canal translates to *ropewalk*. It's a very long canal that provided rope-makers in the 17th century enough space to stretch and twist the ropes they made for the shipbuilding industry in Amsterdam. *Tram: 2 or 5 to Hobbemastraat.*

❷ Spiegelgracht. Turn right onto this short canal lined with antiques shops. There are over 70 specialized antiques dealers in this neighborhood, selling everything from barometers and clocks to brass and copper ornaments. If you choose to stop and have a look, be sure to leave one person in your party with the canal bike—don't leave it unattended.

❸ Prinsengracht. Turn right onto one of Amsterdam's golden-age canals. Many of the houses here were built around 1700. Several of them still have their original neck gables.

❹ Reguliersgracht. Turn left onto Reguliersgracht. You can spot seven identical arched bridges, perfectly aligned, spanning this canal. These date back to the 17th century. It's a lovely place for photographs.

❺ Keizersgracht. Turn left onto Keizersgracht, the city's widest canal at 28m (92 ft.). Many of the houses lining the canal were built as coach houses for the mansions of the prosperous on nearby Herengracht. You'll be pedaling for quite some time (30–45 min.) on Keizersgracht as it winds through the edge of the old center and up toward

You can get a close-up view of houseboats and bridges from the seat of a canal bike.

Keizersgracht.

Centraal Station and into the Jordaan. To begin looping back, turn left on tiny Leliegracht and then left on Prinsengracht.

6 Prinsengracht. You are back on Prinsengracht, but now you are in the heart of the elegant and charming Jordaan neighborhood. The Anne Frank House is here, and the tall spire of the Westerkerk, the largest reformed church in Holland, will be visible to your right. You'll see many houseboats lining the banks of Prinsengracht, most of them have been here since just after World War II, when the housing

Prinsengracht.

shortage forced some people to find alternative dwellings. There are currently some 2,500 houseboats in Amsterdam, and no further permits will be issued for new ones.

7 Looiersgracht. Turn right at the "Tanners' Canal"; not surprisingly, this is where leather used to be tanned.

8 Lijnbaansgracht. Turn left on "Ropewalk Canal," the long canal that you pedaled on earlier.

9 Passeerdersgracht. Turn left here and notice the low railing on the bridge that stops cars from falling into the water. Before the railing was built, cars frequently fell into the canal, and in the 18th century, horses and carriages also tumbled into the water. The railings were not installed until the 1960s—on all 100km (62 miles) of Amsterdam's canals.

10 Prinsengracht & Leidsegracht. Turn right and you're on Prinsengracht again. Turn right onto Leidsegracht. Notice the four houses at nos. 72–78, which display four different kinds of gables: No. 72 has a neck gable, 74 a cornice gable, 76 a spout gable, and 78 a step gable (see the box "Gables 101" on p 51 for a primer on gables).

⑪ Leidsebosje. Turn left and you'll spot the large Art Nouveau American Hotel opposite the mooring. You've reached the end! Return your pedal bikes here.

⑫ ★★ Café Americain. Overlooking the Leidseplein mooring, this turn-of-the-20th-century cafe is a national monument of Dutch Art Nouveau. Legend has it that the infamous spy Mata Hari had her wedding reception here. Don't forget to look up to admire the frosted-glass Tiffany chandeliers. The hamburgers are especially good, served with thick-cut home fries; there are also plenty of salads and sandwiches to choose from. *In the American Hotel, Leidsekade 97.* ☎ *020/556-3232.* $$.

Café Americain.

Canal Bike Rentals & Rules

Canal bikes seat up to five people. They are stable and comfortable. The charge is 8€ per person per hour. The above itinerary will take about 2 hours, a bit longer if you go slowly. You'll need a credit card, a 50€ refundable deposit (which can go on the card), and an ID to rent your canal bike. Rental hours are 10am to 10pm June to September and 10am to 6:30pm the rest of the year. Rent from Canal Bike, at the Rijksmuseum Mooring (☎ 020/626-5574; www.canal.nl). In addition to this mooring, there are spots in front of the Anne Frank House, Leidseplein (facing the American Hotel), and at the corner of Keizersgracht and Leidsestraat. If you get tired, you can always drop off your canal bike at one of these moorings and receive your refundable deposit back.

Always stay to the right in the canals—this is especially important when going under bridges in narrow canals. All other traffic has a right of way. The port area is off-limits to canal bikes. If you need a break, stop at one of the mooring docks. *Never* leave your canal bike unattended—it will be immediately towed away.

The Best of the Outdoors

Biking along the **Amstel River**

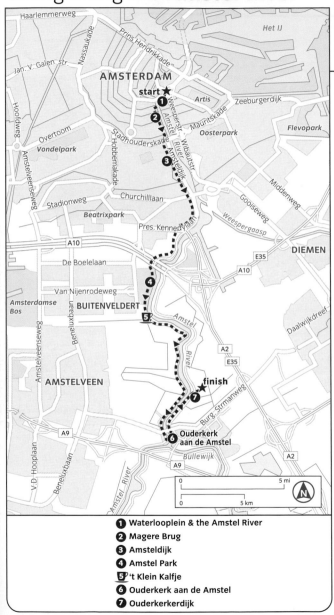

1 Waterlooplein & the Amstel River
2 Magere Brug
3 Amsteldijk
4 Amstel Park
5 't Klein Kalfje
6 Ouderkerk aan de Amstel
7 Ouderkerkerdijk

Amsterdammers go everywhere on their bikes and don't particularly enjoy it when visitors on rented *fiets* (as bikes are called here) attempt to navigate the inner city's complicated streets and alleyways. This bike route takes you away from the city center and out to more pleasant and tranquil surroundings. START: **Tram 9 or 14 to Waterlooplein.**

❶ Waterlooplein & the Amstel River. Once you've rented your bikes (see the box on the next page), head south along the Amstel on Amsteldijk. Keep your eye out for houseboats moored along both banks and for a lot of other boat activity on the river. The Amstel will be to your left; on the return, you'll be on the far bank, with the river on your right.

❷ ★ Magere Brug (Skinny Bridge). The Skinny Bridge over the Amstel is actually an 18th-century replacement of the original 17th-century bridge. It's a double-drawbridge made of African azobe wood. Hundreds of lights illuminate the bridge at night. The Theater Carre, one of the city's largest theaters, is visible from the bridge.

Traveling the city by bike is a way of life for many Amsterdammers.

Enjoy peaceful views of canals and the river as you pedal through the city.

❸ Amsteldijk. As you pedal south, you'll need to cross busy Stadhouderskade. Continue on Amsteldijk south to the Berlage Brug (Berlage Bridge), where the traffic thickens again. Stay on the Amsteldijk—most of the road traffic swings away to the right on President Kennedylaan. The road becomes noticeably quieter, almost rural, and you can relax and admire the many houseboats lined along the banks of the river.

❹ Amstel Park. Go under the highway bridge (A10 Ring Rd.) and continue along the riverbank until you reach this lovely park. There's a statue of Rembrandt and a windmill at the end of the park, so continue pedaling to the south until you see them. It's a classic Dutch scene and perfect for a little rest and a photo or two.

5 't Klein Kalfje. At this point you'll probably want to stretch out your legs and have a snack. This little Dutch cafe/restaurant has a great riverside terrace mere steps from the canal barges moored alongside it. Try the Dutch pea soup or spicy sausages with hot mustard. Consider fueling up for your ride back with a strong Dutch coffee served with sweetened, condensed milk. *Amsteldijk 355.* ☎ *020/644-5338. $.*

6 Ouderkerk aan de Amstel. Continue south, past villas and cottages, to this charming little village. If you have time, lock up your bikes by the river and meander through the village streets before heading back.

You can usually bike for a whole day for under 10€ if you get your bike back to the rental shop before closing time.

7 Ouderkerkerdijk. Head back north on the opposite bank. You'll find this a quieter and narrower road than the Amsteldijk, with much less traffic. When you reach the Berlage Brug again, you'll know

you're getting close to your starting point. The streets are busier here, but stay on the right bank and enjoy the different vistas until you reach Waterlooplein. ●

Renting Your Bikes

The rental outlet closest to your starting point is MacBike at Mr. Visserplein 2 (☎ 020/620-0985; www.macbike.nl). To get there, take tram 9 or 14 to Waterlooplein. You'll need a passport and a 50€ deposit (cash or credit card; the deposit is refundable upon return of the bike). Rates are 4€ for 2 hours, 7€ for 1 day, and 10€ for 24 hours. They are open daily 9am to 5:45pm. The 1-day rental requires you to return the bike by closing time. MacBike rents a range of bikes, including tandems and six-speed touring bikes. There's another MacBike near Centraal Station at Stationsplein 12 (☎ 020/624-8391).

Dining Best Bets

Best **Herring Sandwich**
Van Dobben $ *Reguliersdwarsstraat 5-7-9 (p 100)*

Best **Dining with a View**
Elf $$ *Jonge Roelensteeg 21 (p 96)*

Best **When Money Is No Object**
★★★ La Rive $$$$ *Professor Tulpplein 1 (p 97)*; and ★★★ Excelsior $$$$ *Nieuwe Doelenstraat 2–8 (p 96)*

Best for **Dutch Oysters from Zeeland**
★ Le Pecheur $$$ *Reguliersdwarsstraat 32 (p 97)*

Best for **Dining with Your Shoes Off**
★ Supper Club $$ *Jonge Roelensteeg 21 (p 100)*

Best **Young Celebrity Chef Hot Spot**
★★★ 15 $$$ *Jollemanhof 9 (p 96)*

Best for an **Innovative Five-Course Menu**
★★★ Bordewijk $$$$ *Noordemarkt 7 (p 94)*; and ★★★ Christophe's $$$ *Leliegracht 46 (p 95)*

Best for **Drop-Dead Gorgeous Decor**
★★ The Dylan $$$$ *Keizersgracht 384 (p 96)*

Best for **Upmarket Moroccan Cuisine**
★★ Mamouche $$ *Quellijnstraat 104 (p 98)*

Best for **Trendy Parents with No Babysitter**
★ Bloesem $$ *Binnen Dommerstraat 13 (p 94)*

Best **Traditional Dutch Pea Soup**
Brasserie De Poort $$ *Nieuwezijds Voorburgwal 176–180 (p 94)*

Best **African Culinary Safari**
Pygma-Lion $$ *Nieuwe Spiegelstraat 5A (p 99)*

Best for **Fancy Breakfast or Fabulous English Tea**
★★ Pulitzer $$$ *Keizersgracht 234 (p 99)*

Best for **Fashionistas**
★ Caffe PC $$ *P.C. Hoofstraat 87 (p 95)*

Best for **Dining Alfresco**
★★ De Kas $$$ *Kamerlingh Onneslaan 3 (p 96)*

Best for **Unpretentious Pub Grub**
O'Donnell's $$ *Heinekenplein (p 98)*

Best **Late-Night Chinese**
Nam Kee $ *Zeedijk 111–113 (p 98)*

Best **Elegant Indonesian**
★ Sama Sebo $$ *P.C. Hoofstraat 27 (p 99)*

Try a herring sandwich the way the locals eat them—with onion and pickles.

Museumplein Area **Dining**

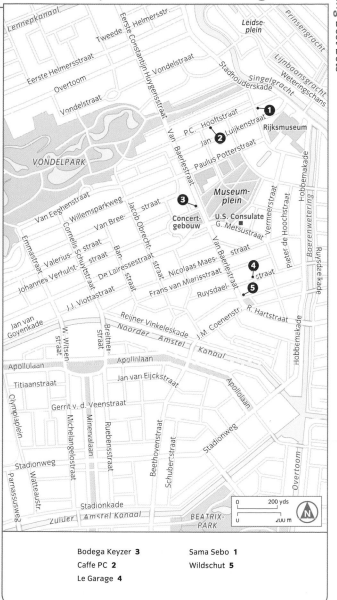

Bodega Keyzer **3**

Caffe PC **2**

Le Garage **4**

Sama Sebo **1**

Wildschut **5**

Central Amsterdam **Dining**

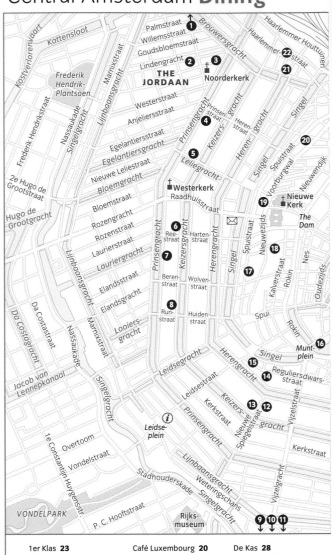

1er Klas **23**

15 **24**

Bloesem **1**

Bordewijk **3**

Brasserie de Poort **19**

Café Luxembourg **20**

Café van Puffelen **7**

Christophe's **5**

De Belhamel **21**

De Duvel **10**

De Kas **28**

The Dylan **8**

Elf **25**

Excelsior **16**

La Rive **27**

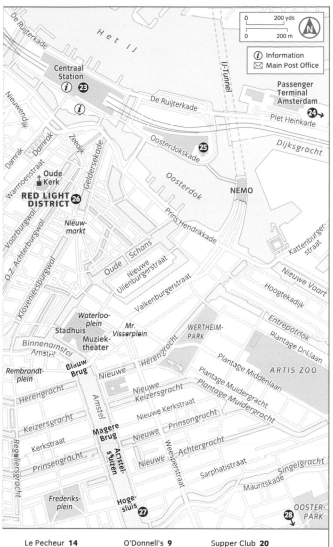

Le Pecheur **14**

Lof **22**

Lucius **17**

Mamouche **11**

Nam Kee **26**

O'Donnell's **9**

Pancake Bakery **4**

Pasta E Basta **13**

Pulitzer **6**

Pygma-Lion **12**

Supper Club **20**

Toscanini **2**

Van Dobben **15**

Amsterdam Restaurants A to Z

★ **kids** **Bloesem** JORDAAN
FUSION Hip and elegant, Bloesem serves up an unusual brand of cuisine: European fusion, with offerings such as garlic soup with chorizo, duck confit with sauerkraut, or a Belgian endive salad with Valencia oranges. This is one of the few trendy Amsterdam eateries that embraces kids. *Binnen Dommerstraat 13.* ☎ *020/770-0407. Entrees 14€–21€. AE, MC, V. Dinner daily. Tram: 16, 24, or 25 to Keizersgracht. Map p 92.*

Bodega Keyzer MUSEUMPLEIN
DUTCH/INTERNATIONAL A classic choice near the Concertgebouw, this 100-year-old restaurant with dark, dusky decor and starched pink linens serves fresh fish, hare, and venison along with the usual international favorites. *Van Baerlestraat 96 (beside the Concertgebouw).* ☎ *020/671-1441. Entrees 20€–33€. AE, DC, MC, V. Breakfast, lunch & dinner Mon–Sat; lunch & dinner Sun. Tram: 3, 5, or 12 to Van Baerlestraat. Map p 91.*

★★★ **Bordewijk** JORDAAN
FRENCH FUSION This trendy restaurant pulls in affluent locals who come here for the creative cuisine, fine cheeses, and superb wine list. If you're a laid-back gourmand, you've found your nirvana, especially in summer, when you can dine alfresco. Specialties include a bouillabaisse Marseillaise with a variety of shellfish and a salted rib roast with bordelaise sauce. There are usually a few Asian-influenced dishes and a sushi-style appetizer. *Noordermarkt 7 (at Prinsengracht).* ☎ *020/624-3899. Reservations required. Entrees 22€–30€. AE, MC, V. Dinner Tues–Sun. Tram: 1, 2, 5, 6, 13, or 17 to Martelaarsgracht. Map p 92.*

Brasserie De Poort OLD CENTER
DUTCH For over a 100 years, this former beer hall has served straightforward Dutch cuisine in a traditional setting complete with Delft blue tiles. Pea soup, lamb, and steaks are the highlights. *In the Hotel Die Port van Cleve, Nieuwezijds Voorburgwal 176–180.* ☎ *020/622-6429. Entrees 16€–23€. AE, DC, MC, V. Breakfast, lunch & dinner daily. Tram: 1, 2, 5, 13, 14, or 17 to the Dam. Map p 92.*

Café Luxembourg OLD CENTER
DUTCH/INTERNATIONAL At one of the most glamorous grand cafes in the city, you'll find a very reasonably

Be sure to sample a variety of Dutch cheeses while you're in Amsterdam.

In summer, you'll find plenty of opportunities to dine alfresco.

priced selection of well-prepared straightforward dishes such as meat-loaf, Indonesian grilled chicken, omelets, salads, and sandwiches. Great for breakfast and lingering over cups of strong coffee with a newspaper. *Spuistraat 22–24 (at Spui).* ☎ *020/620-6264. Entrees 8€–15€. AE, DC, MC, V. Breakfast, lunch & dinner daily. Tram: 1, 2, or 5 to Spui. Map p 92.*

★ **Café van Puffelen** OLD CENTER *DUTCH/INTERNATIONAL* This brown cafe serves delicious dishes with a creative flair, such as fried butterfish with a tarragon-coriander sauce or the house salad with tandoori chicken and Cajun shrimp. Food served until midnight. *Prinsengracht 377.* ☎ *020/624-6270. Entrees 13€–21€. Dinner Mon–Fri; lunch & dinner Sat–Sun. Tram: 13, 14, or 17 to Westermarkt. Map p 92.*

★ **Caffe PC** MUSEUMPLEIN/ VONDELPARK *INTERNATIONAL* Smack dab in the middle of Amsterdam's most elegant shopping street, you can take your place among the absolutely fabulous models and fashion gurus and sip on a martini while indulging in tapas and fresh salads.

P.C. Hoofstraat 87. ☎ *020/673-4752. Entrees 11€–23€. AE, MC, V. Breakfast, lunch & dinner Tues–Sat; breakfast & lunch Sun; lunch only Mon. Tram: 2 or 5. Map p 91.*

★★★ **Christophe's** OLD CENTER *FRENCH/MEDITERRANEAN* Ultra-refined but with a modern flair best describes the cuisine at chef Jean-Christophe Royer's elegant restaurant. The roasted milk-fed Pyrenean lamb in a crust of green peppers and cardamom is one of his specialties. *Leliegracht 46 (between Prinsengracht & Keizersgracht).* ☎ *020/625-0807. Reservations required. Entrees 31€–56€. AE, DC, MC, V. Dinner Tues–Sat. Tram: 6, 13, 14, or 17 to Westermarkt. Map p 92.*

★ **De Belhamel** CANAL BELT *INTERNATIONAL* If you score a window table, you'll have a terribly romantic view of the junction of two canals. The eclectic menu changes often and includes both meat and vegetarian dishes. Appetizers may include puffed pastries layered with smoked salmon, roasted crayfish tails, and steamed mussels. For a main course, the beef tenderloin in Madeira sauce with zucchini rosti and roasted garlic is a specialty. *Brouwersgracht 60 (at Herengracht).* ☎ *020/ 622-1095. Entrees 19€–22€. AE, MC, V. Dinner daily. Tram: 1, 2, 5, 6, 13, or 17 to Martelaarsgracht. Map p 92.*

★ **De Duvel** PIJP *FUSION* Packed with hip and trendy locals, De Duvel (The Devil) serves excellent food in a cozy red dining room. Peanut-pumpkin soup and mushrooms filled with snails are some of the more daring dishes. You'll also find a daily selection of pasta, seafood, and chicken offerings. *1 Van der Helst-straat 59–61.* ☎ *020/675-7517. Entrees 9€–18€. AE, DC, MC, V. Lunch Tues–Sun; dinner daily. Tram: 16, 24, or 25 to Albert Cuypstraat. Map p 92.*

The Dylan restaurant.

★★ De Kas AMSTERDAM SOUTH *INTERNATIONAL* In summer the huge outdoor patio seats over 100 guests adjacent to the fragrant herb gardens. The interior is light and airy (it was formerly a greenhouse) and the menu changes daily. Appetizers may include an eggplant terrine with chèvre and red-pepper coulis; main courses may include a roasted monk-fish with a ratatouille of fresh vegetables from the garden or a leg of lamb with polenta and spinach. If it's in season, try the heavenly rhubarb soup for dessert. *Kamerlingh Onneslaan 3 (close to Amstel Station).* ☎ *020/462-4562. Reservations recommended. Fixed-price lunch 32€; fixed-price dinner 44€. AE, DC, MC, V. Lunch Mon–Fri; dinner Mon–Sat. Tram: 9 to Hogeweg. Map p 92.*

★★ The Dylan JORDAAN *FUSION* This place is ultrachic and ultrahip, not to mention ultraexpensive. Celeb chef Schilo van Coevorden whips up fusion dishes such as foie gras soup with sweet Thai basil or beef with papaya salad. *In The Dylan Hotel, Keizersgracht 384.* ☎ *020/ 530-2010. Reservations required. Entrees 26€–42€. AE, DC, MC, V. Dinner daily. Tram: 6, 13, 14, or 17 to Westermarkt. Map p 92.*

Elf AMSTERDAM EAST *INTERNATIONAL* This place has a stunning view from its 11th-floor perch in a drab-looking building not far from Centraal Station. Unfortunately the food is only mediocre (the potato-leek soup, pasta of the day, and Greek salad are your best bets), but it's worth a stop for drinks and appetizers to enjoy the view. *Oosterdokskade 3–5.* ☎ *020/625-5999. Entrees 13€–21€. AE, MC, V. Lunch & dinner daily. Tram: 1, 2, 4, 5, 6, 9, 13, 16, 17, 24, or 25 to Centraal Station. Map p 92.*

★★★ Excelsior OLD CENTER *FRENCH* Amsterdam's most formal restaurant requires a jacket for men and deep pockets for whoever foots the bill. Crystal chandeliers, crisp linens, and picture windows overlooking the river make for a romantic setting. Expect to dine on such delicacies as foie gras, smoked eel, sweetbreads of lamb, halibut, and veal, all prepared to perfection. *In the Hotel de l'Europe, Nieuwe Doelenstraat 2–8 (facing Muntplein).* ☎ *020/531-1777. Reservations recommended. Entrees 27€–42€; fixed-price menus 60€–78€. AE, DC, MC, V. Breakfast, lunch & dinner Mon–Fri; breakfast & dinner Sat–Sun. Tram: 4, 9, 14, 16, 24, or 25 to Muntplein. Map p 92.*

★★★ 15 AMSTERDAM EAST *INTERNATIONAL* London celebrity chef Jamie Oliver's latest hot spot opened in December 2004 with both a full-menu restaurant and an adjoining trattoria serving less-elaborate (and less-expensive) fare. Drop-dead gorgeous staff, clientele, and food, with dishes like a salad of the day with figs, prosciutto, Gorgonzola, and toasted almonds on field greens; seafood risotto; linguini with horse mushrooms and thyme; or pan-fried calves' liver with balsamic figs and pancetta. *Jollemanhof 9.* ☎ *0900/343-8336. Reservations required for restaurant. Restaurant entrees 29€–38€; trattoria entrees 23€–29€. AE, DC, MC, V. Dinner Mon–Sat. Tram: 10 to Rietlandpark. Map p 92.*

★★★ **La Rive** AMSTERDAM EAST *FRENCH/MEDITERRANEAN* Service at the city's top-rated restaurant can be as stiff as the ironed linens. Nevertheless, you'll dine like royalty on specials like grilled baby abalone with citrus-pickled onion purée or grill-roasted rack of lamb with dates. *In the Amstel InterContinental Hotel, Professor Tulpplein 1 (off Weesperstraat).* ☎ *020/520-3264. Reservations required. Entrees 35€–53€; fixed-price menus 85€–98€. AE, DC, MC, V. Lunch Mon–Fri; dinner Mon–Sat. Tram: 6, 7, or 10 to Sarphatistraat. Map p 92.*

★★★ **Le Garage** MUSEUMPLEIN *FUSION* The hottest restaurant in town serves up creative fusion dishes (such as tuna tartare with curry or a crisp spinach pancake) in a setting with bright lights and big mirrors that's reminiscent of Las Vegas or Tokyo. Call way ahead for dinner reservations or come for lunch when it's quieter. *Ruydaelstraat 54–56 (at Van Baerlestraat).* ☎ *020/679-7176. Reservations required far in advance. Entrees 25€–47€. AE, DC, MC, V. Lunch Mon–Fri; dinner daily. Tram: 3, 5, 12, or 24 to Roelof Hartplein. Map p 91.*

★ **Le Pecheur** OLD CENTER *SEAFOOD* The focus in this airy, tranquil restaurant is less on presentation and more on freshness and taste. Come here for house-smoked salmon, or fresh oysters and mussels from the Dutch province of Zeeland. Extensive wine list. *Reguliersdwarsstraat 32 (behind the Flower Market).* ☎ *020/624-3121. Entrees 22€–40€. AE, MC, V. Lunch Mon–Fri; dinner Mon–Sat. Tram: 1, 2, or 5 to Koningsplein. Map p 92.*

★ **Lof** JORDAAN *FUSION* The menu changes daily depending on what's fresh at local markets. The delicious offerings include one vegetarian specialty. If you're lucky, you'll find the appetizer of white asparagus topped with a poached egg on the menu. For a main course, the roasted cod with black olive and anchovies with capers and pecorino is both delicate and satisfying; the shaved slices

Celebrity chef Jamie Oliver's 15 restaurant.

of leg of lamb on fresh morels is outstanding. Try one of the luscious homemade tortes for dessert. *Haarlemmerstraat 62.* ☎ *020/620-2997. Entrees 12€–22€. No credit cards. Dinner Tues–Sun. Tram: 1, 2, 5, 6, 13, or 17 to Martelaarsgracht. Map p 92.*

Lucius OLD CENTER SEAFOOD
A solid choice for fresh seafood, Lucius offers oysters and lobsters imported from Norway and Canada. The spectacular seafood platter includes mussels, oysters, clams, shrimp, and a half lobster. *Spuistraat 247 (near Spui).* ☎ *020/624-1831. Entrees 20€–40€. AE, DC, MC, V. Dinner daily. Tram: 1, 2, or 5 to Spui. Map p 92.*

★★ Mamouche PIJP MOROCCAN
You'll find exceptionally good Moroccan cuisine in this elegant neighborhood restaurant. Try the lamb tagine with prunes, almonds, olives, and lentils; the rabbit with apricot and cinnamon; or the vegetable couscous. *Quellijnstraat 104.* ☎ *020/673-6361. Entrees 14€–20€. AE, MC, V. Dinner Tues–Sun. Tram: 16, 17, or 24 to Albert Cuypstraat. Map p 92.*

Nam Kee OLD CENTER CHINESE
Don't let the drab, neon-lit dining room dissuade you from trying the very good, fresh food here. Service is fast and they're open late, so you can dine until midnight. I love the duck with plum sauce. *Zeedijk 111–113.* ☎ *020/624-3470. Entrees 6€–13€. AE, MC, V. Lunch & dinner daily. Metro: Nieuwmarkt. Map p 92.*

O'Donnell's PIJP IRISH PUB This boisterous pub, frequented by locals, boasts delicious down-to-earth dishes such as hearty Guinness stew, fish and chips, and grilled lamb chops. There are also several daily specials. *Heinekenplein.* ☎ *020/676-7786. Entrees 11€–19€. AE, MC, V. Lunch & dinner daily. Tram: 16, 24, or 25 to Albert Cuypstraat. Map p 92.*

Pasta E Basta's generous antipasi buffet.

★ 1e Klas OLD CENTER INTERNATIONAL This lovely Art Nouveau restaurant was a waiting room for first-class rail passengers in the late 1800s. Now it's a great place for a drink, a snack, or a full meal, and it's just steps from the trains. The club sandwich and the Caesar salad here are delicious but if you're after a hot meal, the beef stroganoff or the Dover sole with fries are good choices. *Platform 2B, inside Centraal Station.* ☎ *020/625-0131. Entrees 8€–14€. No credit cards. Breakfast, lunch & dinner daily. Tram: 1, 2, 4, 5, 9, 13, 16, 17, 24, or 25 to Centraal Station. Map p 92.*

kids Pancake Bakery JORDAAN
PANCAKES A lovely 17th-century canal warehouse is home to this simple bakery where you can sample yummy pancakes with all kinds of toppings, from curried turkey with pineapple to honey, nuts, and whipped cream. *Prinsengracht 191.* ☎ *020/625-1333. Pancakes 5€–11€. AE, MC, V. Lunch & dinner daily. Tram: 6, 13, 14, or 17 to Westermarkt. Map p 92.*

★ **Pasta E Basta** OLD CENTER
ITALIAN This cozy, candlelit Italian restaurant has the best opera-singing waiters this side of La Scala. The fantastic antipasti buffet is served out of an antique grand piano and the main courses include a delicious Gorgonzola lasagna with Parma ham and fresh basil. *Nieuwe Spiegelstraat 8.* ☎ *020/422-2222. Fixed-price menus 32€. AE, MC, V. Dinner daily. Tram: 1, 2, or 5 to Koningsplein. Map p 92.*

★★ **Pulitzer** JORDAAN *GOURMET*
You'll find this trendy restaurant inside the drop-dead gorgeous Hotel Pulitzer. I recommend coming for the full buffet breakfast, served until 2pm, or afternoon tea complete with crumpets, clotted cream, and cucumber sandwiches. An innovative lunch and dinner menu is also available. *Keizersgracht 234.* ☎ *020/523-5235. Reservations recommended. Entrees 12€–25€. AE, DC, MC, V. Breakfast, lunch & dinner daily. Tram: 13, 14, or 17 to Westermarkt. Map p 92.*

Pygma-Lion CENTER *SOUTH AFRICAN* This airy, attractive eatery invites you to embark on a culinary safari. Unique specials include zebra meatballs with corn and mint sauce, curry-marinated ostrich kabobs, and crocodile steak. There's a great selection of South African wines. *Nieuwe Spiegelstraat 5A.* ☎ *020/420-7022. Entrees 18€–21€. AE, MC, V. Lunch & dinner Tues–Sun. Tram: 1, 2, or 5 to Koningsplein. Map p 92.*

★ **Sama Sebo** MUSEUMPLEIN/VONDELPARK *INDONESIAN* This upmarket Indonesian restaurant is decorated with rush mats and batiks and serves an unrivaled 23-plate *rijsttafel* (a feast consisting of rice and many accompanying dishes like curried meats, fish, vegetables, and nuts) just a few steps from the

The dining room at the Pulitzer.

Rijksmuseum. *P.C. Hoofstraat 27.* ☎ *020/662-8146. Entrees 14€–21€. AE, DC, MC, V. Lunch & dinner Mon–Sat. Tram: 2 or 5 to Hobbemastraat. Map p 91.*

★ **Supper Club** OLD CENTER
FUSION Kick off your shoes inside this ultramodern (and blindingly white) hyper-trendy restaurant, stretch out on couches and cushions, and groove along to whatever the DJ is spinning as you wait for your meal. There's no telling what the chefs (called "food magicians") will whip up—you inform your waiter of any dietary restrictions and wait to see what arrives on your table (typical dishes include pea soup or Parma ham with melon for an appetizer, and seared tuna on greens or chicken with a sweet and sour sauce with roasted vegetables for a main course). The atmosphere and not the food is the highlight here. *Jonge Roelensteeg 21.* ☎ *020/344-6400. Reservations recommended. Entrees 14€–25€. AE, DC, MC, V. Dinner daily. Tram: 1, 2, 5, 13, 14, or 17 to the Dam. Map p 92.*

★ **Toscanini** JORDAAN *ITALIAN*
This small, charming eatery has an open kitchen and a warm and welcoming ambience. Authentic Italian

Some of the 20-odd dishes you might find at an Indonesian rijsttafel.

dishes include veal lasagna, seafood risotto, a selection of fresh fish, and many excellent pastas. *Lindengracht 75 (off Brouwersgracht).* ☎ *020/623-l2813. Entrees 15€–19€. AE, DC, MC, V. Dinner Mon–Sat. Tram: 1, 2, 5, 6, 13, or 17 to Martelaarsgracht. Map p 92.*

kids **Van Dobben** OLD CENTER *DUTCH FAST FOOD* This is more of a sandwich place than a restaurant, but some patrons swear by the platter of giant meatballs. Locals come here for herring, liverwurst, croquets, or ox-tongue sandwiches. Simpler roast beef and Gouda sandwiches are also available. *Reguliers-dwarsstraat 5-7-9.* ☎ *020/624-4200.*

Sandwiches 2.50€–4.50€; entrees 6€–8€. No credit cards. Lunch & dinner daily. Tram: 4, 9, or 14 to Rembrandtplein. Map p 92.

Wildschut MUSEUMPLEIN *INTER-NATIONAL* Wildschut is great any time of day but especially on summer evenings when the large terrace is open. You'll find vegetarian lasagna, large salads, and good sandwiches here, but the people-watching is more interesting than the food. *Roelof Hartplein 1–3 (off Van Baerlestraat).* ☎ *020/676-8220. Entrees 12€–15€. MC, V. Breakfast, lunch & dinner Mon–Fri; lunch & dinner Sat–Sun. Tram: 3, 5, 12, or 24 to Roelof Hartplein. Map p 91.* ●

Nightlife Best Bets

Best Places to **Sip Martinis with the Young & the Beautiful**
★★★ Arc, *Reguliersdwarsstraat 44 (p 106)*; and ★★ Mme. Jeanette, *Van der Helststraat 42 (p 106)*

Best Place to **Drink with the Locals**
★ Café Nol, *Westeerstraat 109 (p 106)*

Friendliest **Gay Bar**
★★ April, *Reguliersdwarsstraat 37 (p 109)*

Best **Irish Pub**
★★ O'Donnell's Irish Pub, *Heinekenplein (p 110)*

Best for **Baggy Jeans & Hip-Hop**
De Duivel, *Reguliersdwarsstraat 87 (p 108)*

Best **Brown Cafe with a Summer Terrace**
★★ Café II Prinsen, *Prinsenstraat 27 (p 107)*

Best **Place to Dance if You're Over the Hill**
Back Door, *Amstelstraat 32 (p 108)*

Most **Hip & Happening Dance Clubs**
★★ Tonight, *'s-Gravesandestraat 51 (p 109)*; and ★★★ Club Panama, *Oostelijke Handelskade 4 (p 108)*

Best for **Romance**
★ Chocolate Bar, *Van der Helststraat 62-A (p 106)*

Best for **Expats**
Three Sisters Grand Pub, *Leidseplein 2 (p 110)*

Best **Lesbian Bar**
★ Vive-la-Vie, *Amstelstraat 7 (p 109)*

Best for **House-Brewed Beer**
★ In de Wildeman, *Kolksteeg 3 (p 107)*

Best for **a Drink after Midnight**
★★★ Club Panama, *Oostelijke Handelskade 4 (p 108)*

Best **Happy Hour**
Hoppe, *Spui 18–20 (p 107)*

See the "Cannabis Tolerance" box on p 110 for information on Dutch coffee shops, another popular nighttime option.

Pijp **Nightlife**

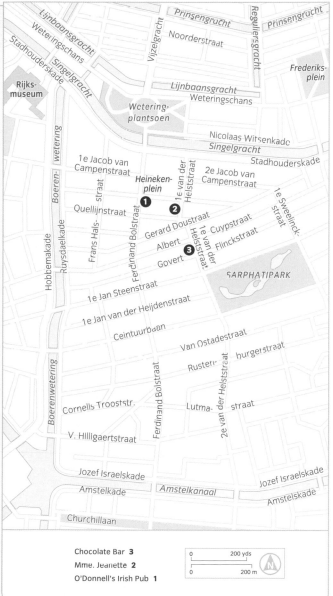

Chocolate Bar **3**

Mme. Jeanette **2**

O'Donnell's Irish Pub **1**

0   200 yds

0   200 m

Central Amsterdam Nightlife

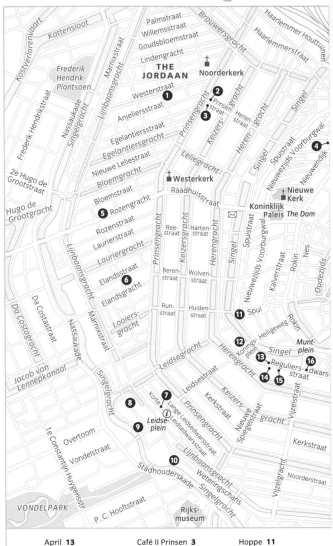

April **13**	Café II Prinsen **3**	Hoppe **11**
Arc **15**	Club Panama **23**	In de Wildeman **4**
Back Door **20**	De Duivel **16**	iT **21**
Café Americain **9**	De Vergulde Gaper **2**	Lux **8**
Café Nol **1**	Escape Venue **17**	Mazzo **5**

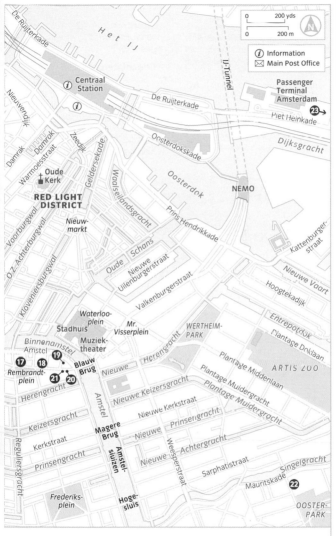

Odeon **12**

Paradiso **10**

Saarein **6**

Sinners in Heaven **19**

Soho Pub **14**

Three Sisters Grand Pub **7**

Tonight **22**

Vive-la Vic **18**

Nightlife A to Z

Bars

★★★ Arc OLD CENTER One of the most attractive and trendy bars in the city pulls in some gay clients as well. The friendly, 20- and 30-something mixed crowd is very hip. Many opt to lounge the night away here and indulge in the delicious appetizer platters. *Reguliersdwarsstraat 44.* ☎ *020/689-7070. Tram: 1, 2, or 5 to Koningsplein. Map p 104.*

★ Café Americain CANAL BELT This Amsterdam institution is a grand place for drinks in the evenings, though be warned that it's frequented heavily by tourists. *Leidsekade 97.* ☎ *020/556-3232. Tram: 1, 2, 5, 6, 7, or 10 to Leidseplein. Map p 104.*

★ Café Nol JORDAAN This cafe is more like a relaxed bar. It caters to a mix of young, cool Jordaaners and old-timers who have lived in the neighborhood for ages. The kitsch interior includes crystal chandeliers, mirrors, a red carpet, and hanging potted plants. Great place to observe young yuppies in action.

Westeerstraat 109. ☎ *020/624-5380. Tram: 3 or 10 to Marnixplein. Map p 104.*

★ Chocolate Bar PIJP The hippest bar in the Pijp also serves up delicious light meals. DJs spin great music on the weekends, and there's a lovely terrace for when the weather's fine. *Van der Helststraat 62-A.* ☎ *020/675-7672. Tram: 16, 24, or 25 to Albert Cuypstraat. Map p 103.*

★★ Lux CANAL BELT Leidseplein is quite touristy, but the lovely Lux draws in a healthy dose of locals with its laid-back chic attitude. Sit on the upper level to enjoy a sweeping view of the place. *Marnixstraat 403.* ☎ *020/422-1412. Tram: 1, 2, 5, 6, 7, or 10 to Leidseplein. Map p 104.*

★★ Mme. Jeanette PIJP The young well-heeled crowd sinks into plush sofas and sips martinis while DJs spin the latest music at this trendy place. The food's good, too, and there's a pleasant summer terrace where you can lounge alfresco. *Van der Helststraat 42.* ☎ *020/673-3332. Tram: 16, 24, or 25 to Albert Cuypstraat. Map p 103.*

The average price for a beer in Amsterdam is 1.50€ to 3€ (hip clubs and hotel bars will likely charge more).

Brown cafes get their name from their smoke-stained walls.

Brown Cafes

★★ Café II Prinsen JORDAAN

This attractive brown cafe has mosaic-tiled floors and a wood muraled ceiling. I like to while away a warm evening on the enchanting summer terrace overlooking Prinsengracht. There's usually a healthy mix of local intellectuals and visitors, from young backpackers to middle-aged professionals. *Prinsenstraat 27.* ☎ *020/624-49722. Tram: 1, 2, 5, 6, 13, or 17 to Martelaarsgracht. Map p 104.*

De Vergulde Gaper CANAL BELT

On warm nights the lovely terrace right beside the Prinsengracht is the place to be for 30- and 40-something professionals, and the interior is cozy, too, decorated with vintage posters and old medicine bottles (it used to be a pharmacy). *Prinsenstraat 30.* ☎ *020/624-8975. Tram: 1, 2, 5, 6, 13, or 17 to Martelaarsgracht. Map p 104.*

Hoppe OLD CENTER

This historic brown cafe, dating back to 1670, has a convivial, smoky atmosphere. It's often crowded, especially with the after-work crowd, so expect standing room only in the early evenings. It gets rowdy here when the professionals leave; most of the patrons who end up staying late are young students traveling around

Europe while driving heavily. *Spui 18–20.* ☎ *020/420-4420. Tram: 1, 2, or 5 to Spui. Map p 104.*

★ In de Wildeman OLD CENTER

This historic brown cafe originated in 1690 and has its original tile floor and rows of bottles from when it functioned as a distillery. It boasts 17 draft and 200 bottled beers from around the world. It's a laid-back atmosphere, with mostly hard-drinking but very friendly locals ranging from 30- to 50-something. *Kolksteeg 3.* ☎ *020/638 2318. Tram: 1, 2, 5, 6, 13, or 17 to Nieuwezijds Kolk. Map p 104.*

A friendly neighborhood brown cafe can be a great place to mix with locals.

Pick up a copy of What's On in Amsterdam *at the tourist office for the scoop on Amsterdam's hottest clubs.*

Dance Clubs

Back Door CANAL BELT   This place fills up very late (well after midnight on weekends) with a fun-loving over-25 crowd who come here for funk, soul, and a good mix of '60s and '70s music. *Amstelstraat 32.* ☎ *020/620-2333. Cover 5€–8€. Tram: 4, 9, or 14 to Rembrandtplein. Map p 104.*

★★★ Club Panama EAST   A historic 1899 building that used to be a power station houses this hip club. The attractive bar/restaurant in the lobby opens up into the cavernous Club Panama, which hosts big-name DJs and special events, depending on the day and seasons. This is a see-and-be seen place for the 30- to 40-something professionals. So dress to impress and bring some attitude. Call ahead for program information. *Oostelijke Handelskade 4.* ☎ *020/ 311-8686. www.panama.nl. Cover 10€–22€. Tram: 10 to Rietlandpark. Map p 104.*

De Duivel CANAL BELT   Amsterdam's coolest hip-hop club plays both "rap oldies" and contemporary hip-hop. The crowd is young and the dress code is drooping jeans—the baggier the better. *Reguliersdwarsstraat 87.* ☎ *020/850-2400. No cover. Tram: 16, 24, or 25 to Keizersgracht. Map p 104.*

★ Escape Venue OLD CENTER   Three dance floors, a great sound system, and a healthy mix of local and international DJs make this one of the prime choices for the young and trendy. Saturday is especially popular. *Rembrandtplein 11.* ☎ *020/622-1111. Cover 8€–20€. Tram: 4, 9, or 14 to Rembrandtplein. Map p 104.*

★ iT CANAL BELT   Some nights this club is more gay than straight, but everybody always has a great time, especially if you're young and enjoy house and techno. Occasional drag shows. Very trendy crowd. *Amstelstraat 24.* ☎ *020/625-0111. Cover 8€–12€. Tram: 4, 9, or 14 to Rembrandtplein. Map p 104.*

Mazzo JORDAAN   Small, friendly, and intimate, Mazzo is a longtime favorite with an all-ages crowd, a traditional disco with a compact dance floor and flashing lights. *Rozengracht 114.* ☎ *020/626-7500. Cover 8€–12€. Tram: 6, 13, 14, or 17 to Westermarkt. Map p 104.*

Odeon CANAL BELT   Inside this converted 17th-century canal house, you'll find period ceiling paintings and stucco decor. You'll also find three dance floors, each offering a different kind of music: classic disco, jazz, and house. *Singel 460.* ☎ *020/ 624-9711. Cover 3€–6€. Tram: 1, 2, or 5 to Koningsplein. Map p 104.*

Paradiso CANAL BELT   An old church has been transformed into this majestic club, with lofty ceilings and high balconies encircling the dance floor. Big-name DJs and theme nights help make this place appealing to a variety of stylish

people. *Weteringschans 6–8.*
☎ *020/626-4521. www.paradiso.nl.*
Cover 8€–22€. Tram: 1, 2, 5, 6, 7, or
10 to Leidseplein. Map p 104.

Sinners in Heaven CANAL BELT
This ultratrendy place tends to
attract Dutch celebrities (mostly
TV stars) and offers a mix of
music depending on the night—
everything from R & B to hip-hop
and swing. *Wagenstraat 3–7.*
☎ *020/620-1375. Cover 6€–12€.*
Tram: 4, 9, or 14 to Rembrandtplein.
Map p 104.

★★ **Tonight** EAST   The city's
hottest club is in the ultratrendy
Hotel Arena. Talented DJs keep
everybody happy with a mix of
music from the '60s to the '90s. A
youngish, well-dressed crowd flocks
here, especially on weekends after
midnight. *'s-Gravesandestraat 51.*
☎ *020/850-2400. www.hotel*
arena.nl. Cover 6€–10€. Tram: 7
or 10 to Kore 's-Gravesandestraat.
Map p 104.

Gay & Lesbian
★★ **April** OLD CENTER   The
bright, loud front room feels like a
pub, the back room, with its dimly lit
bar, has a more cruisy feel. If you're
a gay man looking to meet some

local folks, this should be your first
stop—very happening for happy
hour but the action dies down after
11pm. *Reguliersdwarsstraat 37.*
☎ *020/625-9572. Tram: 1, 2, or 5 to*
Koningsplein. Map p 104.

Saarein JORDAAN   This is a
longtime favorite with lesbians,
though it's increasingly drawing a
mixed crowd. A great location in
the Jordaan makes it appealing
to locals. Convivial atmosphere.
Elandstraat 119. ☎ *020/623-4901.*
Tram: 7, 10, or 17 to Marnixstraat.
Map p 104.

★ **Soho Pub** OLD CENTER   Open
until 4am on weekends (3am week-
days), this place doesn't get going
until late (after 11pm) and is the city's
quintessential gay pub. *Reguliersd-*
warsstraat 36. ☎ *020/422-3312.*
Tram: 1, 2, or 5 to Koningsplein.
Map p 104.

★ **Vive-la-Vie** OLD CENTER   Open
for more than 25 years, this is the
place for lesbians in Amsterdam.
The crowd is young and lively,
and lipstick isn't forbidden. Very
popular in the early evenings. *Ams-*
telstraat 7. ☎ *020/624-0114. Tram:*
4, 9, or 14 to Rembrandtplein. Map
p 104.

Hotel Arena's Tonight club.

Pubs

★★ O'Donnell's Irish Pub PIJP

This neighborhood Irish pub pulls in many of the young, up-and-coming professionals who live in the Pijp. It's a happy, boisterous place where the Guinness is good and the bartenders are Irish and friendly. The food is excellent, too. *Heinekenplein.* ☎ *020/676-7786. No cover. Tram: 16, 24, or 25 to Albert Cuypstraat. Map p 103.*

Three Sisters Grand Pub CANAL

BELT   Popular with the throngs of visiting Brits, this is a good place to come for a pint of English lager or warm ale. Especially busy for happy hour. *Leidseplein 2.* ☎ *020/428-0428. No cover. Tram: 1, 2, 5, 6, 7, or 10 to Leidseplein. Map p 104.* ●

Order a colaatje pils (co-la-che pilss) if you want beer in a small glass, or a bakkie or vass if you'd like a large.

Cannabis Tolerance

Amsterdam's reputation as a wild party town is a direct result of its tolerance towards cannabis. But the practice is technically illegal and only just tolerated. Local producers are allowed to operate so long as they don't go in for large-scale production (some of their wares are used for pain relief), and individuals are only allowed to carry up to 30 grams (about 1 oz.) for personal use. Coffee shops in Amsterdam are not places to get a meal, they're places where a customer can purchase marijuana or hashish. They are licensed and controlled and provide a place where patrons can sit and smoke all day if they so choose—and the coffee actually is not bad. Coffee shops are not allowed to sell alcohol, and only some serve food (usually very light snacks). Warmoesstraat, on the fringe of the Red Light District, is lined with coffee shops, making it the prime spot for coffee-shop crawls by bands of young tourists looking for a good time (they're usually dazed by the end of the evening, as you can imagine, so things are actually quite mellow). One of the friendlier places is **Coffeeshop Sheeba,** Warmoesstraat 73 (☎ 020/512-3127), open daily 9am to 1am.

Arts & Entertainment
Best Bets

Best for **Laughing the Night Away**
Boom Chicago, *Leidseplein 12* *(p 116)*

Best **Chamber Orchestra**
★★ Beurs van Berlage, *Beursplein 1* *(p 116)*

Best for **Controversial Movies**
★ De Balie Film & Cultural Center, *Kleine-Gartmanplantsoen 10 (p 117)*

Best **Acoustics**
★★★ Concertgebouw, *Concertgebouwplein 2–6 (p 116)*

Best **Contemporary Concert Space**
★ Heineken Music Hall, *Arena Blvd. 590 (p 117)*

Best for **Opera**
★ Muziektheater, *Waterlooplein 22* *(p 117)*

Best for **Gay & Lesbian Plays**
Melkweg, *Lijnbaansgracht 234A* *(p 120)*

Best for **Lavish Musicals**
★ Carre, *Amstel 115–125 (p 119)*

Best for **Ballet**
★ Muziektheater, *Waterlooplein 22* *(p 117)*

Best for **Modern Dutch Theater**
★ Staddsschouwburg, *Leidseplein 26 (p 120)*

Best **Blues Venue**
Maloe Melo, *Lijnbaansgracht 163* *(p 118)*

Best for **Experimental Jazz**
★★ Muziekgebouw, *Piet Heinkade 1* *(p 117)*

Best **Free Concerts**
★★ Vondelpark Openluchttheater, *Vondelpark (p 117)*

The Muziektheater.

Museumplein Area **A&E**

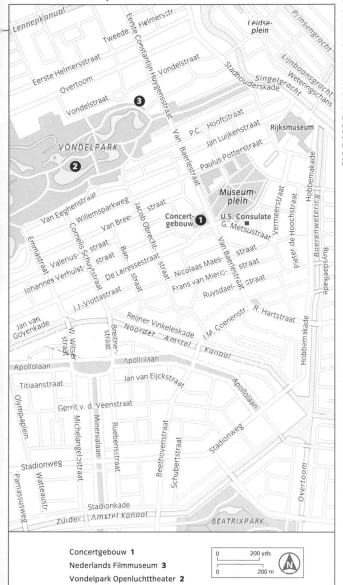

Concertgebouw **1**
Nederlands Filmmuseum **3**
Vondelpark Openluchttheater **2**

| 0 | 200 yds |
| 0 | 200 m |

Central Amsterdam **A&E**

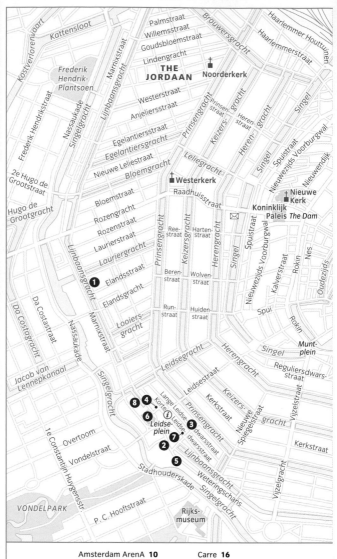

Amsterdam ArenA **10**	Carre **16**
Bananenbar **13**	Casa Rosso **14**
Beurs van Berlage **11**	De Balie Film &
Boom Chicago **4**	Cultural Center **2**
Bourbon Street **3**	Heineken Music Hall **9**

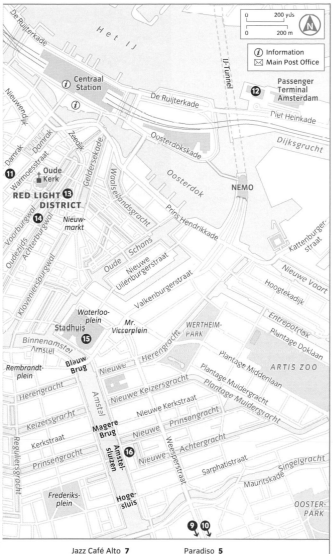

Jazz Café Alto **7**
Maloe Melo **1**
Melkweg **8**
Muziekgebouw **12**
Muziektheater **15**

Paradiso **5**
Staddsschouwburg **6**

Arts & Entertainment A to Z

Classical Music

★★ Beurs van Berlage OLD CENTER The former home of the Amsterdam Stock Exchange (built in 1903) is now a concert venue with two halls. It's home to the Netherlands Philharmonic Orchestra and the Netherlands Chamber Orchestra. *Beursplein 1.* ☎ *020/624-0141. www.beursvanberlage.nl. Tickets 8€–22€. Tram: 4, 9, 14, 16, 24, or 25 to the Dam. Map p 114.*

★★★ Concertgebouw MUSEUMPLEIN The Concert Building, home of the Royal Concertgebouw Orchestra, first opened its doors in 1888 and is touted as one of the most acoustically perfect concert halls in the world. The world's greatest orchestras, ensembles, conductors, and soloists regularly perform here. There are two halls, a main hall and a recital hall, which hosts smaller ensembles, like chamber orchestras. Each hall hosts a daily performance, making the venue one of the busiest concert halls in the world. *Concertgebouwplein 2–6.* ☎ *020/671-8345. www.concertgebouw.nl. Tickets*

A performance at the Concertgebouw.

15€–100€; Aug summer concerts 30€. Tram: 3, 5, or 12 to Museumplein; 16 to Concertgebouwplein. Map p 113.

Comedy Theater

Boom Chicago CANAL BELT Amsterdam's premier comedy theater has been going strong for over a decade, with lots of improvisational shows. Most performances are in English. Good fun. *Leidseplein*

Musicians rehearse at the Muziekgebouw.

Theater, Leidseplein 12. ☎ 020/423-0101. www.boomchicago.nl. Tickets 12€–32€. Tram: 1, 2, 5, 6, 7, or 10 to Leidseplein. Map p 114.

Concerts
Amsterdam ArenA SOUTHEAST From sports (soccer, mostly) to big-name rock concerts, the city's biggest events take place at this giant arena, located in southeast Amsterdam. *ArenA Blvd., Amsterdam Zuidoost.* ☎ 020/311-1313. www.amsterdam arena.nl. Tickets 15€–60€. Metro: Strandvliet/ArenA. Map p 114.

★ **Heineken Music Hall** SOUTH-EAST   Near the giant Amsterdam ArenA, the smaller Heineken Music Hall hosts more intimate concerts. Performers have included Moby, Duran Duran, the Black Eyed Peas, Michael Bolton, Marilyn Manson, and Anita Baker, among others. *Arena Blvd. 590* ☎ 020/311-3871. www.heinekenmusichall.nl. Tickets 30€–62€. Subway: Strandvliet/ArenA. Map p 114.

★★ **Muziekgebouw** EAST   The city's fabulous new concert hall opened in June 2005 just east of Centraal Station. It's the hub of experimental music and jazz in Amsterdam and home to Bimhuis, the city's premier jazz, blues, and improvisational venue featuring top local and international musicians. *Piet Heinkade 1.* ☎ 020/788-2010. www.muziekgebouw.nl & www.bimhuis.nl. Tickets 10€–60€. Tram: 26 to Muziekgebouw. Map p 114.

Paradiso CANAL BELT   This old church has been transformed to present an eclectic variety of music. It's a great place for dance events on weekends, but it also doubles as a concert venue for big-name artists. The Rolling Stones, David Bowie, and Prince have all played here. *Weteringschans 6–8.* ☎ 020/626-4521. www.paradiso.nl. Tickets

The National Ballet and Netherlands Dance Theater, both highly regarded, perform at the Muziektheater.

8€–22€. Tram: 1, 2, 5, 6, 7, or 10 to Leidseplein. Map p 114.

★★ **Vondelpark Open-luchttheater** MUSEUMPLEIN This open-air venue comes to life on certain nights during July and August, when pop, rock, Latin, or classical artists give free concerts in the midst of peaceful, green Vondel-park. Bring a picnic and enjoy an enchanting evening under the stars. *In Vondelpark.* ☎ 020/523-7790. Free admission. Tram: 2 or 5 to Hobbemastraat. Map p 113.

Dance & Opera
★ **Muziektheater** EAST   One of the city's stellar performance venues has a superbly equipped 1,600-seat auditorium and is the home base of the highly regarded Netherlands Opera and National Ballet. The acclaimed Netherlands Dance Theater, based in The Hague, also performs here regularly. *Waterlooplein 22.* ☎ 020/625-5455. www.hetmuziek theater.nl. Tickets 20€–80€. Tram: 9 or 14 to Waterlooplein. Map p 114.

Film
★ **De Balie Film & Cultural Center** CANAL BELT   This all-purpose cultural center has an eclectic calendar of workshops, lectures,

and film festivals. You can see controversial and award-winning features and documentaries and lots of interesting movies from around the world that don't make it to mainstream theaters. *Kleine-Gartmanplantsoen 10.* ☎ *020/553-5100. www.debalie. nl. Movie tickets 7€; lectures 6€–10€. Tram: 1, 2, 5, 6, 7, or 10 to Leidseplein. Map p 114.*

★ Nederlands Filmmuseum

MUSEUMPLEIN   Much more than just a museum, this striking venue is located inside the magnificent Vondelpark and features two theaters (one of them with a fabulous Art Deco interior) that schedule interesting retrospectives and film festivals. *Vondelpark.* ☎ *020/589-1400. www.filmmuseum.nl. Tickets 7.80€. Tram: 2 or 5 to Hobbemastraat. Map p 113.*

Jazz

Bourbon Street CANAL BELT   In this intimate cafe, you'll find excellent local jazz, blues, soul, and funk. Well-known groups from the U.S. and Europe play here, too. This place is hopping until well after midnight. *Leidsekruisstraat 6–8.* ☎ *020/623-3440. No cover, except for special acts (10€). Tram: 1, 2, 5, 6, 7, or 10 to Leidseplein. Map p 114.*

Jazz Café Alto CANAL BELT   Top-notch quartets play nightly in this small cafe, with the occasional blues band mixed in. On Wednesday evenings the noted saxophonist Hans Dulfer plays, sometimes accompanied by his equally well-regarded daughter Candy. *Korte Leidsedwarsstraat 115.* ☎ *020/626-3249. No cover. Tram: 1, 2, 5, 6, 7, or 10 to Leidseplein. Map p 114.*

Maloe Melo JORDAAN   This small club presents live blues most nights, interspersed with evenings of jazz and country, and jams on Tuesday and Thursday nights. Big-name musicians are featured occasionally as well. *Lijnbaansgracht 163.* ☎ *020/420-4592. Cover 4€. Tram: 7, 10, or 17 to Elandsgracht. Map p 114.*

Sex Shows

Bananenbar OLD CENTER   Bananas are the featured props in the nightly sex shows here. The audience (which tends toward hormone-driven young men) is encouraged to participate. *Oudezijds Achterburgwal 37.* ☎ *020/622-4670. Tram: 1, 2, 4, 5, 6, 9, 13, 16, 17, 24, or 25 to Centraal Station. Map p 114.*

Casa Rosso OLD CENTER   In its own words, Casa Rosso puts on "one of the most superior Erotic shows in

The Nederlands Filmmusem shows a wide variety of films throughout the year, including some English-language films.

Jazz lovers have a number of excellent venues to choose from in Amsterdam.

the world, with a tremendous choreography and a high-level cast." You may not describe it in those words, but this live sex show joint is very popular with throngs of visiting young men. *Oudezijds Achterburgwal 106–108.* ☎ *020/627-8943. Tram: 4, 9, 14, 16, 24, or 25 to the Dam. Map p 114.*

Theater

★ **Carre** CANAL BELT This big, plush theater used to be a full-time circus arena. Now it hosts the most lavish Dutch-language (and some English) productions of top Broadway and London musicals such as *Les Miserables* and *Miss Saigon.* Several international opera, modern

Buying Tickets

The most convenient ticket outlet in the city is the **Amsterdam Uit Buro (AUB) Ticketshop** located at Leidseplein 26 (☎ 0900/0191; www.uitburo.nl; tram: 1, 2, 5, 6, 7, or 10). Here you can reserve and purchase tickets for any venue in town and also pick up a plethora of brochures, pamphlets, and schedules for any cultural event in Amsterdam, including film festivals and temporary exhibits at galleries and museums. There's a charge of 2€ per ticket, but you may consider it worth the time you'll save by not having to chase down tickets on your own. This office also allows you to purchase tickets and make reservations before leaving home via their website. For phone reservations using a credit card, they are open daily from 9am to 9pm. The office itself is open Monday to Wednesday and Saturday from 10am to 6pm, Thursday from 10am to 9pm, and Sunday from noon to 6pm.

The **VVV Amsterdam** tourist information office (p 166) can also reserve tickets, but they usually have a longer wait time and they charge 2.50€ per ticket. If you are staying at an upmarket hotel, I suggest calling the concierge (even before you leave home) to arrange for reservations.

The Carre theater hosts lavish productions of Dutch plays as well as top Broadway and London shows.

dance, and ballet companies also perform here on occasion. *Amstel 115–125.* ☎ *020/622-5225. www. theatercarre.nl. Tickets 12€–125€.*

Staddsschouwburg.

Tram: 6, 7, or 10 to Weesperplein. Map p 114.

Melkweg CANAL BELT   This large contemporary multidimensional venue includes a theater, cinema, concert hall, photo gallery, and exhibition space. Its theater tends to showcase new groups, both international and local, with emphasis on experimentalism. Comedy, multicultural, and gay and lesbian plays are staged here, too. Most performances are in Dutch. *Lijnbaansgracht 234A.* ☎ *020/531-8181. www. melkweg.nl. Tickets 5€–10€. Tram: 1, 2, 5, 6, 7, or 10 to Leidseplein. Map p 114.*

★ **Staddsschouwburg** CANAL BELT   This 950-seat municipal theater is the city's main venue for mainstream Dutch theater and the occasional play in English, both classic and modern. Opera and ballet performances are also occasionally staged here. *Leidseplein 26.* ☎ *020/ 624-2311. www.staddsschouwburg amsterdam.nl. Tickets 10€–45€. Tram: 1, 2, 5, 6, 7, or 10 to Leidseplein. Map p 114.* ●

9 The Best **Lodging**

Lodging Best Bets

The Agora.

Museumplein Area **Lodging**

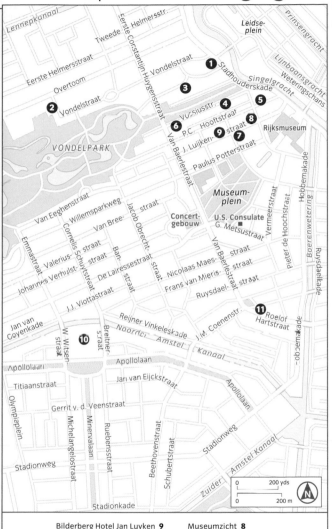

Bilderberg Hotel Jan Luyken **9**	Museumzicht **8**
The College **11**	Owl Hotel **3**
Hilton Amsterdam **10**	P.C. Hooft **7**
Hotel De Filosoof **2**	Piet Hein **6**
Hotel Smit **5**	Vondelpark Museum
Marriott **1**	Apartments and B&B **4**

Central Amsterdam **Lodging**

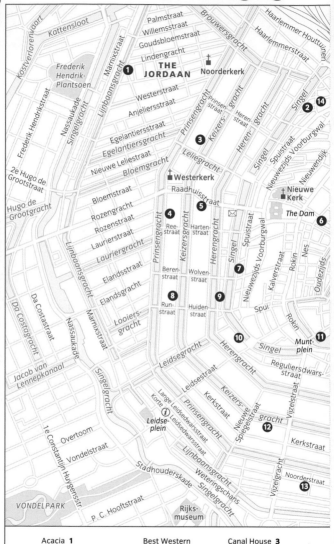

Acacia **1**	Best Western Eden **18**	Canal House **3**
Agora **10**		Clemens **5**
Ambassade Hotel **9**	Best Western Lancaster **23**	The Dylan **8**
Amstel Intercontinental Amsterdam **22**	Bridge Hotel **21**	Hoksbergen **7**
		Hotel Arena **24**

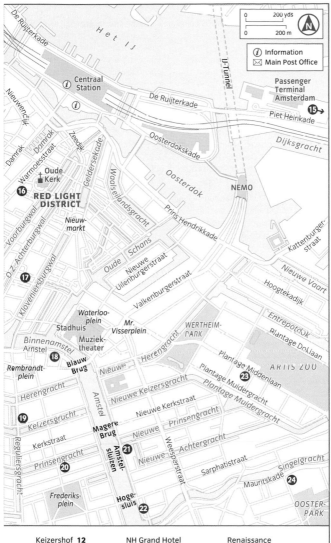

Keizershof **12**

L'Europe **11**

Lloyd Hotel **15**

Mercure Amsterdam
Arthur Frommer **13**

NH Grand Hotel
Krasnapolsky **6**

Prinsenhof **20**

Pulitzer **4**

Radisson SAS Hotel **17**

Renaissance
Amsterdam **14**

Seven Bridges **19**

Singel Hotel **2**

Winston **16**

Amsterdam Hotels A to Z

★ **Acacia** JORDAAN   Simple, clean rooms, friendly owners, and a good location (on a small canal close to many trendy restaurants) make this small hotel a standout. All rooms have canal views, but there's no elevator. For an authentic Amsterdam living experience, rent one of the hotel's two nearby houseboats. *Lindengracht 251.* ☎ *020/622-1460. www.hotelacacia.nl. 18 units (including houseboats). Doubles 80€–90€ w/breakfast; houseboat 95€–110€ double. MC, V. Tram: 3 or 10 to Marnixplein. Map p 124.*

Agora CANAL BELT   Great location and friendly service make this small hotel a good value. Rooms are small (except for family rooms, which are quite spacious) and are outfitted with mahogany and antiques. Rooms overlooking the canal can be somewhat noisy, so if you're a light sleeper, ask for a room in back, with views of a pretty garden. There's no elevator. *Singel 462.* ☎ *20/627-2200. www.hotelagora.nl. 16 units. Doubles 150€ w/breakfast. AE, DC, MC, V. Tram: 1, 2, or 5 to Koningsplein. Map p 124.*

Sleeping quarters at the Agora.

★ **Ambassade Hotel** CANAL BELT Ten elegant 17th- and 18th-century canal houses have been renovated to create this perfectly located gem. Individually decorated rooms are furnished in Louis XV and XVI styles. You'll find free Internet and bike rental on the premises. Not all rooms are accessible by elevator, so be sure to specify your needs when booking. *Herengracht 335–353.* ☎ *020/555-0222. www.ambassade-hotel.nl. 124 units. Doubles 188€–195€. AE, MC, V. Tram: 1, 2, or 5 to Spui. Map p 124.*

★★★ **Amstel InterContinental Amsterdam** CANAL BELT   The grande dame of Dutch hotels since its opening in 1867 is still top-notch both in luxurious accommodations and superior customer service. Plush, elegant rooms come with Italian-marble bathrooms. There's a gorgeous indoor pool alongside the modern health club, with steam room and sauna. The hotel's restaurant, La Rive (p 97), is one of the best in the city. *Prof. Tulpplein.* ☎ *020/622-6060. www.interconti. com. 79 units. Doubles 490€–580€. AE, DC, MC, V. Tram: 6, 7, or 10 to Weesperplein. Map p 124.*

One of the Bilderberg Hotel's sophisticated, modern rooms.

★ **Best Western Eden** OLD CENTER   Across the river from the Muziektheater, this hotel offers promotional rates as low as 80€ off season—an excellent value for Amsterdam. Even at full price, this hotel does not disappoint, with bright, modern, spacious rooms (some with lovely river views) and a friendly staff. *Amstel 144.* ☎ *020/530-7888. www.edenhotelgroup. com. 340 units. Doubles 160€–210€. AE, DC, MC, V. Tram: 4 or 9 to Rembrandtplein. Map p 124.*

kids **Best Western Lancaster** EAST   A stone's throw from Artis Zoo, this is a great location for families, away from the hustle and bustle of the old center, but just a 10-minute tram ride or 30-minute walk away. The quietest neighborhood in Amsterdam is also a short walk from the Tropenmuseum and the Botanical Gardens. Attractive triple rooms are perfect if you're traveling with kids. *Plantage Middenlaan 48.* ☎ *020/530-7888. www.edenhotel group.com. 92 units. Doubles 130€–172€. AE, MC, V. Tram: 9 or 14 to Plantage. Map p 124.*

★ **Bilderberg Hotel Jan Luyken** MUSEUMPLEIN   Steps from the Rijksmuseum, this charming small hotel is located on a leafy residential street. The attractive rooms feature a sophisticated, modern decor and are

meticulously maintained. With amenities such as 24-hour room service and in-room massage, this place feels like a large, full-service hotel without the crowds. *Jan Luijkenstraat 58.* ☎ *020/573-0730. www.janluyken.nl. 62 units. Doubles 220€–295€. AE, DC, MC, V. Tram: 2 or 5 to Hobbemastraat. Map p 123.*

★ **Bridge Hotel** CANAL BELT   The riverfront location and large, simply furnished but comfortable rooms make this hotel a great value. Two new airy and spacious apartments (250€–275€) boast large picture windows and are great for families. The full Dutch breakfast served every morning is a nice touch. *Amstel 107–111.* ☎ *020/623-7068. www.the bridgehotel.nl. 36 units. Doubles 95€–130€ w/breakfast. AE, DC, MC, V. Tram: 6, 7, or 10 to Westerplein. Map p 124.*

★ **Canal House** CANAL BELT Three adjoining 1630 canal homes make up this charming hotel. The thoughtfully renovated rooms feature antiques and Chinese rugs. Luckily, the 17th-century breakfast room was not gutted and is a wonderful place to start your day. *Keizersgracht 148.* ☎ *020/622-5182. www.canalhouse.nl. 26 units. Doubles 140€–190€ w/breakfast. DC, MC, V. Tram: 6, 13, 14, or 17 to Westermarkt. Map p 124.*

Clemens JORDAAN This small, tidy hotel is operated by a mother-daughter team who take personal care of the comfortable rooms. Nos. 7 and 8 have balconies facing the Westerkerk. All rooms come with a small refrigerator. *Raadhuisstraat 39.* ☎ *020/624-6089. www.clemenshotel. nl. 9 units, 5 with bathroom. Doubles 85€ with bathroom, 75€ without bathroom. AE, MC, V. Tram: 13, 14, or 17 to Westerkerk. Map p 124.*

★★ **The College** MUSEUMPLEIN Opened in March 2005, this modern boutique hotel is housed in a former school building, thus the name. It's just a short walk from the major museums. Expect to see plenty of trendy 30-something European professionals here. *Roelof Hartstraat 1.* ☎ *020/571-1511. www.thecollege hotel.com. 43 units. Doubles 180€–250€. AE, DC, MC, V. Tram: 3, 5, 12, or 24 to Roelof Hartplein. Map p 123.*

★★★ **The Dylan** CANAL BELT Formerly called Blakes, this is Amsterdam's most lavish boutique hotel, located in a historic 17th-century building on one of the city's most scenic canals. Modern elegance reigns here, with four-poster beds and spacious bathrooms. Each

A suite at the College.

room is individually decorated with rich fabrics and bold colors. Service is superb and discreet enough for celebrities. *Keizersgracht 384.* ☎ *020/530-2010. www.dylan amsterdam.com. 41 units. Doubles 390€–690€. AE, DC, MC, V. Tram: 1, 2, or 5 to Spui. Map p 124.*

★ **Hilton Amsterdam** SOUTH The infamous room 902 is where John Lennon and Yoko Ono had their "Bed in for Peace" in 1969. The designers of the hotel consulted Yoko when renovating the room, and it now features extensive use of natural materials only. Modern facilities

The Manhattan suite at the Dylan.

and a good location, within walking distance from the Rijksmuseum. *Apollolaan 138.* ☎ *020/710-6000. www.amsterdam.hilton.com. 271 units. Doubles 215€–315€. AE, DC, MC, V. Tram: 5 or 24 to Apollolaan. Map p 123.*

Hoksbergen CANAL BELT This attractive budget hotel is housed in a 300-year-old canal house and offers small but bright and (very) clean rooms at affordable rates. Rooms at the front have canal views. There's no elevator. *Singel 301.* ☎ *020/626-6043. www.hotelhoksbergen.com. 14 units. Doubles 72€–104€ w/breakfast. AE, DC, MC, V. Tram: 1, 2, or 5 to Spui. Map p 124.*

★ **Hotel Arena** EAST What used to be an orphanage dating back to 1890 is now a stylish hotel catering mostly to European yuppies who love the spare modern rooms, each individually decorated by up-and-coming Dutch designers. There's a casual eatery called To Dine and a bar called To Drink. The hotel's nightclub, Tonight (p 109), is housed in the old orphanage chapel. *'s-Gravesandestraat 51.* ☎ *020/850-2410. www.hotelarena.nl. 121 units. Doubles 100€–175€ w/breakfast. AE, DC, MC, V. Tram: 7 or 10 to Kore 's-Gravesandestraat. Map p 124.*

Hotel De Filosoof MUSEUMPLEIN In a leafy and upscale residential neighborhood not far from Vondelpark, you'll find this small, friendly hotel. Rooms are small but charming, and some are very bright, with large wood-framed windows. They're individually decorated in themes that reflect various philosophies (like the Golden Age–style Spinoza room, or the simply decorated Thoreau room). A great value, especially if you want peace and quiet. It's about a 10-minute walk to the center of the city. *Anna van den Vondelstraat 6.*

☎ *020/683-3013. www.hotelfilosoof. nl. 50 units. Doubles 105€–138€ w/breakfast. AE, MC, V. Tram: 1 to Jan Pieter Heijestraat. Map p 123.*

Hotel Smit MUSEUMPLEIN Steps from all the elegant shops on P.C. Hoofstraat, this hotel offers comfortable, if slightly small, rooms at a reasonable price. The Smit's best feature is the lovely Café Van Gogh on its ground floor, offering reasonably priced homemade meals in a trendy setting. Breakfast here (not included in room rates) features delicious Gouda omelets, Dutch pancakes, and fresh croissants. *P.C. Hoofstraat 24.* ☎ *020/662-9161. www.hotelsmit.nl. 106 units. Doubles 104€–135€. MC, V. Tram: 2 or 5 to Hobbemastraat. Map p 123.*

Keizershof CANAL BELT This four-story canal house dates back to 1672. A grand piano in the hotel's lounge adds a certain stateliness to the place. Rooms are beamed and cozy with simple, modern furnishings, but only two have private bathrooms. In summer you can enjoy a delicious Dutch breakfast in the lovely

Hotel Arena's rooms feature sleek, modern design.

flower-filled courtyard. There's no elevator. *Keizersgracht 618.* ☎ *020/622-2855. www.hotelkeizershof.nl. 6 units, 2 with bathroom. Doubles with bathroom 90€–105€; without bathroom 65€; all w/breakfast. MC, V. Tram: 16, 24, or 25 to Spui. Map p 124.*

★★★ **L'Europe** OLD CENTER
This classic luxury hotel, a member of the Leading Hotels of the World, commands a prime riverside location. The rooms are plush, spacious, and bright, and all boast marble bathrooms. There are two highly acclaimed restaurants (including Excelsior, p 96) and a lovely summer terrace overlooking the Amstel. *Nieuwe Doelenstraat 2–8.* ☎ *020/531-1777. www.leurope.nl. 100 units. Doubles 350€–450€. AE, DC, MC, V. Tram: 4, 9, 14, 16, 24, or 25 to Spui. Map p 124.*

★★★ **Lloyd Hotel** EAST   This historic Amsterdam School–style hotel opened in 2004 in the up-and-coming Eastern Docklands neighborhood after a major renovation. It boasts a wide variety of rooms—from basic to luxury. Choose from tiny rooms without baths (at 80€) to impressive suites and duplexes (one even has a grand piano and a sweeping staircase). Most rooms are outfitted by

One of Lloyd Hotel's basic rooms.

contemporary Dutch architects and designers. There's an excellent restaurant on the premises. *Oostelijke Handelskade 34.* ☎ *020/561-3636. www.lloydhotel.com. 120 units, 106 with bathroom. Doubles without bathroom 80€; doubles with bathroom 140€–320€. AE, DC, MC, V. Tram: 10 or IJ-tram to Rietlandpark. Map p 124.*

★★ **Marriott** MUSEUMPLEIN
Commanding a fantastic location between Leidseplein and Vondelpark, this Marriott has been meticulously renovated with firm mattresses, fluffy comforters, and a

L'Europe's impressive exterior.

A Canal-House Warning

Elevators are difficult things to shoehorn into the cramped confines of a 17th-century canal house and cost more than some moderately priced and budget hotels can afford. Many simply don't have them. If lugging your old wooden sea chest up six flights of steep, narrow, hard-to-navigate stairs is liable to void your life insurance, better make sure an elevator is in place and working. Should there be no such amenity and you have trouble climbing stairs, ask for a room on a low floor.

new gym featuring the latest workout equipment. The friendly staff goes out of their way to provide for your comfort, and the talented concierge is a great source of help for both tourist and business information. *Stadhouderskade 12.* ☎ *020/607-5555. www.marriott. com. 392 units. Doubles 229€–381€. AE, DC, MC, V. Tram: 1, 2, 5, 6, 7, or 10 to Leidseplein. Map p 123.*

Mercure Amsterdam Arthur Frommer CANAL BELT This small, friendly hotel once owned by Arthur Frommer is tucked away off Vijzelgracht. The newly renovated rooms are not huge but are very stylish, with soft pastel colors. There's a cozy bar. *Noorderstraat 46.* ☎ *020/622-0328. www.accorhotels.com. 90 units. Doubles 120€–155€. AE, DC, MC, V. Tram: 16, 24, or 25 to Prinsengracht. Map p 124.*

Museumzicht MUSEUMPLEIN This basic hotel is housed in a Victorian house just across from the Rijksmuseum. Rooms are small but clean, decorated with an eclectic mix of antique furnishings. There's no elevator and the steps are quite steep. *Jan Luijkenstraat 22.* ☎ *020/671-2954. www.hotel museumzicht.nl. 14 units, 3 with bathroom. Doubles 95€ with bathroom; 70€ without bathroom; all*

w/breakfast. AE, DC, MC, V. Tram: 2 or 5 to Hobbemastraat. Map p 123.

NH Grand Hotel Krasnapolsky OLD CENTER Smack in the midst of it all, the "Kras" (as it's known locally) faces the Royal Palace and is an Amsterdam landmark. The sizes and shapes of the rooms vary considerably and the upkeep on them is iffy. Renovations are progressing somewhat haphazardly; ask for a newly renovated room when you make your reservation. *Dam 9.* ☎ *020/ 554-9111. www.nh-hotels.com. 468 units. Doubles 300€–350€. AE, DC, MC, V. Tram: 4, 9, 14, 16, 24, or 25 to the Dam. Map p 124.*

Owl Hotel MUSEUMPLEIN This solid bargain choice is just a few minutes' walk from Leidseplein, but in a quiet spot. Rooms are fairly compact, with oak furnishings and whitewashed walls. There's a bar and a small garden, great for lounging on a warm summer day. *Roemer Visscherstraat 1.* ☎ *020/618-9484. www.owl-hotel.nl. 34 units. Doubles 98€–145€ w/breakfast. AE, DC, MC, V. Tram: 1, 2, or 5 to Leidseplein. Map p 123.*

P.C. Hooft MUSEUMPLEIN Smack in the middle of the city's most elegant shopping street, this small hotel has bright and tidy rooms but only three come with private bathrooms. For such a low price, you may overlook the inconvenience of using the clean public bathrooms down the hall. *P.C. Hooftstraat 63.* ☎ *020/662-7107. 16 units. Doubles 65€ with bathroom, 55€ without bathroom; all w/breakfast. MC, V. Tram: 2 or 5 to Hobbemastraat. Map p 123.*

★ **Piet Hein** MUSEUMPLEIN The most modern and attractive reasonably priced hotel in Amsterdam boasts a refreshing "nautical" decor in all of its stylish rooms. The deluxe rooms—located in a recently renovated wing of the hotel—come with air-conditioning, which is unusual for a hotel in this price range. There's a comfortable bar/lounge where you can unwind in the evenings. *Vossiusstraat 52–53.* ☎ *020/662-7205. www.hotelpiethein.com. 65 units. Doubles 120€–165€ w/breakfast. AE, DC, MC, V. Tram: 3, 5, or 12 to Van Baerlestraat. Map p 123.*

Prinsenhof CANAL BELT This recently renovated canal house offers basic but comfortable rooms with beamed ceilings. Front rooms look out onto the Prinsengracht, where colorful houseboats are moored. There's no elevator, but a pulley hauls your luggage up and down the stairs. *Prinsengracht 810.* ☎ *020/623-1772. www.hotel prinsenhof.com. 10 units, 4 with bathroom. Doubles 80€ with bathroom; 60€ without bath; all w/breakfast. AE, MC, V. Tram: 4 to Prinsengracht. Map p 124.*

★★★ **Pulitzer** JORDAAN The Pulitzer offers its lucky guests pure luxury without being ostentatious. A divine location on a canal at the edge of the Jordaan, rooms so plush you sink into them, and a fantastic restaurant (p 99) make this the ideal place to splurge on a romantic getaway. *Prinsengracht 315–331.* ☎ *020/523-5235. www.starwood. com. 230 units. Doubles 470€–545€. AE, DC, MC, V. Tram: 13, 14, or 17 to Westermarkt. Map p 124.*

Radisson SAS Hotel OLD CENTER This sprawling hotel is close to everything. There are four room categories, so be sure to state your preference when you reserve. The Dutch rooms come with oak furnishings and orange curtains; the Scandinavian, Asian, and Art Deco rooms are sparser and airier. The hotel has a full restaurant and a bar that serves light meals. *Rusland 17.* ☎ *020/623-1231. www.radissonsas.com. 243*

The cozy bar at the Pulitzer.

A room at the Renaissance Amsterdam.

units. Doubles 230€–330€. AE, DC, MC, V. Tram: 4, 9, 14, 16, 24, or 25 to Spui. Map p 124.

★★ Renaissance Amsterdam

OLD CENTER The Renaissance is a standout among the city's large business hotels, tucked away off a charming canal just a 5-minute walk from Centraal Station. It feels much cozier than you'd expect from its size. Rooms are very spacious, with picture windows and large bathrooms, and staff go out of their way to help. *Kattengat 1.* ☎ *020/621-2223. www.renaissance hotels.com. 405 units. Doubles*

149€–345€. AE, DC, MC, V. Tram: 1, 2, 5, 13, or 17 to Martelaarsgracht. Map p 124.

★ Seven Bridges CANAL BELT

This canal-house gem is meticulously maintained. Each individually decorated room boasts antique furnishings (Art Deco, Biedermeier, Louis XVI, rococo), handmade Italian drapes, and wood-tiled floors. Attic rooms have sloped ceilings and exposed wood beams. *Reguliersgracht 31.* ☎ *020/623-1329. 8 units. Doubles 120€–220€ w/breakfast. MC, V. Tram: 4 to Keizersgracht. Map p 124.*

Money-Saving Tips

Amsterdam's hotels can be expensive. There are around 30,000 hotel and hostel beds available, 40% of which are in four- and five-star hotels. The Netherlands adheres to the Benelux Hotel Classification System, which awards stars to hotels based on set criteria—having a pool, an elevator, and so forth. The hotel with the most stars is not necessarily the most comfortable or elegant (though often it is). Each establishment must display a sign indicating its classification, from "1" for those with minimum amenities to "5" for deluxe, full-service hotels. The city has moved in recent years to redress the balance in favor of hotels in the mid- and low-priced categories, but it is inevitably a slow process. If a particular hotel strikes your fancy but is out of your price range, it may pay to inquire if special off-season, weekend, specific weekday, or other packages will bring prices down to what you can afford. Many hotels offer significant rate reductions between November 1 and March 31, with the exception of the Christmas and New Year period.

Summer Stays: Reserve Ahead

July and August are tough months for finding hotel rooms in Amsterdam. Try to reserve as far ahead as possible for this period. If you have problems getting a room, contact the tourist information office, which can generally arrange a room somewhere though it might not be in the kind of hotel you are looking for and you might need to pay more for a room in a better-class hotel.

You can also reserve with the **Amsterdam Reservation Center** (☎/fax 077/700-0888; http://res.amsterdamtourist.nl); and with the **Netherlands Reservations Center (NRC),** Nieuwe Gouw 1, 1442 LE, Purmerend, Netherlands (☎ **0299/689-144;** fax 0299/689-154; www.hotelres.nl).

Singel Hotel OLD CENTER   Three canal houses were united to create this bright and welcoming hotel, conveniently located near Centraal Station. A few of the modern, spacious rooms have an attractive view of the Singel canal. *Singel 13–17.* ☎ *020/626-3102. www.singelhotel. nl. 32 units. Doubles 120€–150€ w/breakfast. AE, DC, MC, V. Tram: 1, 2, 4, 5, 9, 13, 16, 17, 24, or 25 to Centraal Station. Map p 124.*

★★★ Vondelpark Museum Apartments and B&B MUSE-UMPLEIN   Affable Mrs. Fontijn owns this 1879 mansion overlooking lovely Vondelpark. She rents out three apartments at amazing bargain rates (they sleep up to four people) and one charming double bedroom on the ground floor on a B&B basis. All the units come fully equipped with antique furniture and large windows with park views; the top-floor apartment has its own private rooftop terrace. There's no elevator. *Vossiusstraat 14.* ☎ *020/679-8607. 4 units, 3 with bathroom. Doubles 75€ w/breakfast; apt 95€. No credit cards. Tram: 2 or 5 to Hobbema-straat. Map p 123.*

Winston OLD CENTER   Young party-goers flock to this vibrant budget hotel with two bars and a nightclub on the premises. It's on Amsterdam's oldest (and perhaps seediest) street, mere steps from the Red Light District. Families may want to look elsewhere, but it's a great choice for hedonists. *Warmoesstraat 129.* ☎ *020/623-1380. www.winston.nl. 69 units, 25 with bathroom. Doubles 105€ with bathroom; 85€ without bathroom; all w/breakfast. AE, DC, MC, V. Tram: 4, 9, 14, 16, 24, or 25 to the Dam. Map p 124.* ●

Vondelpark Apartments and B&B offers park views at bargain prices.

Haarlem

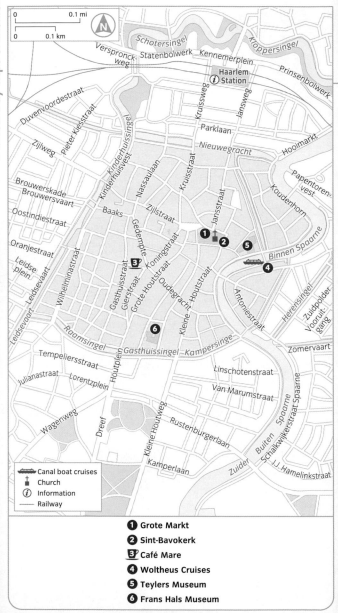

0.1 mi
0.1 km

Schotersingel
Kloppersinge/
Versprronck-weg
Statenbolwerk
Kennemerplein
Prinsenbolwerk
Haarlem
(i) Station
Duvenvoordestraat
Parklaan
Kruisweg
Jansweg
Hooimarkt
Zijlweg
pieter Kiesstraat
Nieuwegracht
Papentoren-vest
Kinderhuissingel
Koudenhorn
Brouwerskade
Brouwersvaart
Nassaulaan
Kinderhuisvest
Kruisstraat
Oostindiestraat
Baaks
Zijlstraat
Jansstraat
Binnen Spaarne
Oranjestraat
Gedempte
Koningstraat
Grote-Houtstraat
Oudegracht
Kleine-Houtstraat
Antoniestraat
Herensingel
Zuidpolder
Vooruit-gang
Leidse
plein
Wilhelminastraat
Gasthuisstraat
Gierstraat
Leidsevaart
Raamsingel
Gasthuissingel
Kampersinge
Zomervaart
Tempeliersstraat
Houtplein
Linschotenstraat
Julianastraat
Lorentzplein
Van Marumstraat
Wagenweg
Dreef
Kleine Houtweg
Rustenburgerlaan
Spaarne
Buiten Spaarne
Kamperlaan
Zuider
Schalkwijkerstraat Spaarne
J.J. Hamelinkstraat

Canal boat cruises
† Church
(i) Information
Railway

1 Grote Markt
2 Sint-Bavokerk
3 Café Mare
4 Woltheus Cruises
5 Teylers Museum
6 Frans Hals Museum

Haarlem, a lovely town of 150,000 inhabitants, is where Frans Hal, Jacob van Ruisdael, and Pieter Saenredam (contemporaries of Rembrandt) lived and painted their famous portraits, landscapes, and church interiors. Haarlem boasts one of the country's best museums and churches, but it has a rural feel, and the lively market in the main square gives you a taste of life in a traditional Dutch village. If you're traveling with kids, be sure to take a canal-boat cruise.

❶ ★★★ **Grote Markt.** A 10-minute walk from the graceful Art Nouveau railway station brings you to the beautiful central market square. The monumental buildings around the tree-lined square, which date from the 15th to 19th centuries, are a visual minicourse in the development of Dutch architecture. The oldest building is Haarlem's 14th-century Stadhuis (Town Hall), a former hunting lodge that was rebuilt in the 17th century. *Market open daily 10am–5pm.*

❷ ★★★ **Sint-Bavokerk (St. Bavo's Church).** Completed in 1520, this lovely church has a rare unity of structure and proportion. The elegant wooden tower is covered with lead sheets and adorned with gilt spheres. The light and airy interior has whitewashed walls and

St. Bavo's famed Christian Muller organ.

sandstone pillars. But the most fascinating aspect of this church is the magnificent, soaring Christian Muller organ, built in 1738. It has 5,068 pipes and is nearly 30m (98 ft.) tall. Mozart played the organ in

Grote Markt.

Haarlem Basics

For many Amsterdammers, Haarlem is not only the closest charming town for an afternoon of shopping at the market, it's also home. Commuters crowd the trains to Haarlem in the early evening, but during the day the twice-hourly trains are close to empty. The trip from Amsterdam's Centraal Station takes just 15 minutes, and the one-way fare is 3.20€. Once in Haarlem, you can pretty much walk everywhere. Haarlem's Centraal Station is just a 10-minute walk from the market square and most of the attractions listed here.

For information, **VVV Haarlem,** Stationsplein 1, 2011 LR Haarlem (☎ **0900/616-1600;** fax 023/534-0537; www.vvvzk.nl), is just outside the rail station. The office is open October to March, Monday to Friday from 9:30am to 5:30pm and Saturday from 10am to 2pm; April to September, Monday to Friday from 9:30am to 5:30pm and Saturday from 10am to 4pm.

1766 when he was just 10 years old, and Handel and Liszt both made special visits here to play it. You can hear the organ in a free concert Tuesday at 8:15pm from May to October; in July and August there's an additional free concert on Thursday at 3pm. From May to October, church services using the organ take place Sunday at 10am; June to October there's an additional 7pm Vespers and Cantata service.
🕐 *45 min. Oude Groenmarkt 23.* ☎ *023/553-2040. Admission 1.50€. Mon–Sat 10am–4pm.*

3 ★ **Café Mare.** This tiny cafe, popular with locals, serves hearty lunches like a Hong Kong noodle soup and lighter fare such as the delicious olive-tapenade sandwich with Gouda cheese. The Tuscan tomato soup with freshly baked bread is also divine. *Warmoesstraat 7.* ☎ *023/551-4112. $.*

4 ★★ **kids Woltheus Cruises.** A canal cruise is an ideal way to get to know Haarlem. The jetty is on the

Spaarne River beside the Gravenstenenbrug, a handsome lift bridge. Boats leave every hour for a cruise around the canals. You'll see loads of historical buildings, and pass close to an 18th-century traditional Dutch windmill—a great photo op.
🕐 *1½ hr. At the Spaarne River & the Gravenstenenbrug.* ☎ *023/535-7723. www.woltheuscruises.nl. Tickets 7€ adults, 4€ children 4–11,*

The Teylers Museum.

Frans Hals's A Banquet of the Officers of the St. George Militia.

free for children under 4. Apr–Oct boats leave at 10:30am, noon, 1:30, 3 & 4:30pm.

5 Teylers Museum. This quirky but interesting museum was the first museum to open in the Netherlands, in 1784. The museum is named after the 18th-century merchant Pieter Teyler van der Hulst, who willed his entire fortune for the advancement of both art and science. You'll find a diverse collection here: drawings by Michelangelo, Raphael, and Rembrandt (which are shown in rotation); fossils, minerals, and skeletons; and instruments of physics and an odd assortment of inventions, including the largest electrostatic generator in the world (built in 1784) and a 19th-century radarscope. ⏱ *1½ hr. Spaarne 16.* ☎ *023/531-9010. www.teylersmuseum.nl. 5.50€ adults; 1€ children under 18; free for children under 5. Tues–Sat 10am–5pm; Sun & holidays noon–5pm.*

6 ★★★ Frans Hals Museum. This magnificent museum is the highlight of many Dutch art lovers' trips to Holland. The 1608 building was once a majestic home for retired gentlemen. Consequently, the famous paintings by Frans Hals (1580–1686) and other masters of the Haarlem School hang in settings that look like the 17th-century houses they were intended to adorn. Hals earned his living by painting portraits of members of the local Schutters (Musketeers) Guild. Typified by his *A Banquet of the Officers of the St. George Militia* (1616), five such works, whose style inspired van Gogh, hang in the museum, along with six more paintings by Hals. Among other pieces is a superb dollhouse from around 1750, and fine collections of antique, silver, porcelain, and clocks. ⏱ *1½ hr. Groot Heiligland 62.* ☎ *023/511-5775. www.franshalsmuseum.com. Admission 5.40€, free for visitors under 19. Tues–Sat 11am–5pm; Sun & holidays noon–5pm.*

The Hague & **Scheveningen**

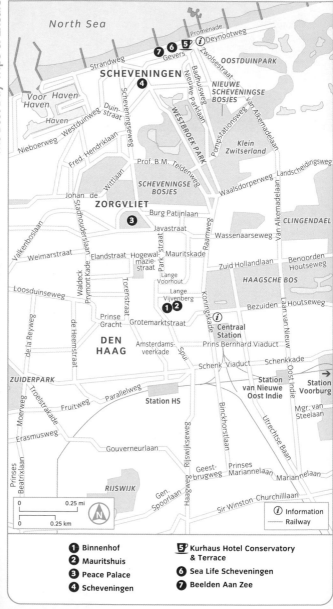

North Sea

Promenade
Deynootweg
Strandweg
Gevers
OOSTDUINPARK
SCHEVENINGEN
Zwolsestraat
Badhuisweg
Nieuwe Parklaan
NIEUWE
SCHEVENINGSE
BOSJES
Voor Haven
Haven
Duinweg
Westduinweg
Scheveningseweg
Duin-straat
Haven
WESTBROEK PARK
Pompstationsweg
van Alkemadelaan
Nieboerweg
Fred. Hendriklaan
Klein
Zwitserland
Prof. B.M. Teldenweg
Witlaan
SCHEVENINGSE
BOSJES
Waalsdorperweg
Landscheidingsweg
Johan de
Stadhouderslaan
ZORGVLIET
Burg Patijnlaan
CLINGENDAEL
Van Alkemadelaan
Valkenboslaan
Weimarstraat
Elandstraat
Javastraat
Hogewal-
mazie-
straat
Mauritskade
Park straat
Wassenaarseweg
Zuid Hollandlaan
Benoorden
Houtseweg
Loosduinseweg
Waldeck
Prymont Kade
de Heemstraat
Torenstraat
Lange
Voorhout
Lange
Vijvenberg
Koningskade
Raamweg
HAAGSCHE BOS
Bezuiden
Houtseweg
Laan van Nieuw
Prinse
Gracht
Grotemarktstraat
**DEN
HAAG**
Amsterdams-
veerkade
Spui
Centraal
Station
Prins Bernhard Viaduct
Schenk Viaduct
Schenkkade
ZUIDERPARK
de la Reyweg
Parallelweg
Station HS
Binckhorstlaan
Station
van Nieuwe
Oost Indie
Oost Indie
Station
Voorburg
Troelstrakade
Moerweg
Fruitweg
Erasmusweg
Gouverneurlaan
Rijswijkseweg
Haagweg
Geest-
brugweg
Prinses
Mariannelaan
Mariannelaan
Mgr. van
Steellaan
Utrechtse Baan
Prinses
Beatrixlaan
RIJSWIJK
Gen.
Spoorlaan
Sir Winston Churchilllaan

0   0.25 mi
0   0.25 km
N

(i) Information
—— Railway

❶ Binnenhof
❷ Mauritshuis
❸ Peace Palace
❹ Scheveningen

❺ Kurhaus Hotel Conservatory
   & Terrace
❻ Sea Life Scheveningen
❼ Beelden Aan Zee

The capital of the Netherlands is stately and grand, and its sister city Scheveningen provides a lovely seaside escape. A day here affords you a fantastic opportunity to visit the Peace Palace, home of the International Court of Justice, and the Binnenhof, the grand home of the Dutch Parliament. It's only an hour away from Amsterdam, but you may consider spending a night here to have some beach time. Some savvy travelers choose to end their trip here or in Rotterdam, 20 minutes away, and fly out from the well-served and very compact Rotterdam Airport that lies between the two cities.

1 ★★★ Binnenhof (Inner Court). A 10-minute tram ride from The Hague's Centraal Station brings you to the city center and this beautiful complex of Parliament buildings. You can join a tour to visit the lofty, medieval Riderzaal (Hall of the Knights); the queen delivers a speech from the throne in this hall each year. Depending on the volume and urgency of government business, you may be able to tour one or the other of the two chambers of the Staaten Generaal (States General), the Dutch Parliament. 🕐 2 hr. Binnenhof 8A. ☎ 070/364-6144. Admission 3€. Guided tours (the only way you can visit) are given hourly Mon–Sat 10am–4pm. Be sure to call ahead to reserve a tour & to confirm availability. Occasionally tours are canceled because of government matters. During school

Binnenhof, home to the Dutch Parliament.

Vermeer's famous Girl with a Pearl Earring.

holidays the tours fill up quickly & you may have to wait several hours if you don't have a booking. Tram: 1 from Centraal Station to Binnenhof.

2 ★★★ Mauritshuis. Adjacent to the Binnenhof complex is this elegant Italian Renaissance–style museum. The villa was built in 1644 as the home of Count Johan Maurits van Nassau, a young court dandy and cousin of the Oranje-Nassaus. Today this small palace houses the Koninklijk Kabinet van Schilderijen (Royal Cabinet of Portraits) and is the permanent home of an impressive art collection given to the Dutch nation by King Willem I in 1816. Highlights include 13 Rembrandts, 3 Frans Hals, and 3 Vermeers (including the famous View of Delft and the beautiful Girl with a Pearl Earring). The museum's three floors are packed with hundreds of other famous works by such painters as Bruegel, Rubens, Steen, and Holbein (including his famous portrait of

Jane Seymour, third wife of Henry VIII of England). If you love the old masters, this museum will take your breath away. ⏱ *1½ hr. Korte Vijverberg 8. ☎ 070/302/3435. www. mauritshuis.nl. Admission 7.50€, free for visitors under 19. Tues–Sat 10am– 5pm; Sun & holidays 11am–5pm. Tram: 1 to Binnenhof.*

❸ ★★★ Peace Palace. You'll have to call ahead for a tour reservation, but this will be the highlight of your trip to The Hague. Andrew Carnegie donated over a million dollars to the construction of this magnificent mock-Gothic Palace, home to the Permanent Court of Arbitration and the International Court of Justice. The building was designed by French architect Louis Cordonnier and completed in 1913. On the tour you'll be able to visit most of the rooms and marvel at gifts given by each of the participating 96 countries: crystal chandeliers (each weighing 1,750kg/ 3,858 lb.) from Delft, made with real rubies and emeralds; incredible mosaic floors from France; 140 kinds of different marble from Italy; a huge Turkish carpet woven in 1926 in Izmir; and an immense 3,500-kilogram

The Peace Palace.

(7,716-lb.) vase from Czar Nicolas of Russia. If the courts are not in session, your guide will take you inside the International Court of Justice, which handles all of the United Nations' judicial cases. ⏱ *1½ hr. Carnegieplein 2. ☎ 070/302-4242. www.vredespaleis.nl. Admission 7.50€. Tours are given Mon–Fri at 10 & 11am & 2, 3 & 4pm. Reservations are required & it's not possible to visit the palace on your own.*

❹ ★★★ Scheveningen. This relaxed, beachside town is only a

The Hague Basics

The Hague is an hour from Amsterdam's Centraal Station. Trains leave every half-hour and stop first at Amsterdam's Schiphol Airport before continuing on to The Hague. The one-way fare is 7.60€. Once you arrive in The Hague, you'll find trams adjacent to the railway station. You can use any Amsterdam tram tickets you might have here, too. Otherwise, you'll pay 1.60€ to 2.30€ depending on your destination; the conductor will sell you a ticket onboard. Tram 1 goes all the way to Scheveningen and back; in the opposite direction, it travels all the way to Delft. The trip from Scheveningen back to The Hague's railway station takes 20 minutes.

For information, **VVV Den Haag,** Koningin Julianaplein, 2500 CD Den Haag (☎ **0900/340-3505;** fax 070/347-2102; www.denhaag. com), is in front of Centraal Station. The office is open Monday to Saturday from 9am to 5:30pm and Sunday from 11am to 5pm.

15-minute tram ride from the center of The Hague. It has wide, sandy beaches and a beautiful pier affording great views of the North Sea. Pleasant cafes line the seaside boardwalk, and on summer weekends sun worshippers fill the beach. Towering over the town and the beach is the majestic Kurhaus Hotel. Consider having a drink in the grand lobby or even a meal at one of the two restaurants, which have fine views of the water. If you're in the mood for some outdoor activity, you can take a long walk over the rolling sand dunes that dot the coast for miles. Turn right as you leave the hotel and in just 10 minutes you'll feel as if you're in the middle of nowhere. *Tram: 1.*

5 ★★★ Kurhaus Hotel Conservatory & Terrace. I like to have a drink or a snack here while enjoying the gorgeous views out to the North Sea. If you're here on a cold afternoon, consider having the traditional English tea in the ultragracious lobby with its tremendously high ceiling and elaborate artwork. *Gevers Deynootplein 30.* ☎ *070/416-2636. Conservatory & terrace open daily 10am–10pm; English tea Mon–Fri 3–6pm. $$$.*

6 ★★ kids Sea Life Scheveningen. This large aquarium has a walk-through underwater tunnel that lets you observe the denizens of the deep, including sharks swimming around above your head. *Strandweg (also known as the boardwalk) 13.* ☎ *070/354-2100. www.sealife.nl. Admission 9.50€ adults, 6€ children 3–11, free for children under 3. Open Sept–June daily 10am–6pm; July–Aug daily 10am–8pm.*

7 ★★★ Beelden Aan Zee. The highlight of your trip to Scheveningen may be this breathtaking

sculpture museum. Opened in 1994, the museum, designed by architect Wim Quist, is built into the sand dunes just steps from the busy boardwalk and blends perfectly with the environment. Take some time to admire the construction and the fantastic use of natural light that spills into the main hall. Terraces overlooking the sea are strewn with amazing sculptures and the indoor galleries look out onto the sand dunes and the sea beyond. Most of the sculptures are of human figures and the sculptors hail from all over the world. One of my favorites is the marble *Venus (asleep)* by Dutch sculptor Jan Meefout. There are also several temporary exhibits during the year, highlighting contemporary sculptors from around the world. Outside the museum, on the boardwalk, you'll find the *Fairy Figures by the Sea,* a permanent extension, open to the public free of charge. The huge, cartoonlike sculptures are all by New Yorker Tom Otterness. Leave some time to stroll around after you visit, admiring the sculptures from the pier and the beach. ⏱ *1½ hr. Hartevelstraat 1.* ☎ *070/ 358-5857. www.beeldenaanzee.nl. Admission 7€. Open Tues–Sun 11am–5pm.*

Scheveningen's colorful street scene.

Delft

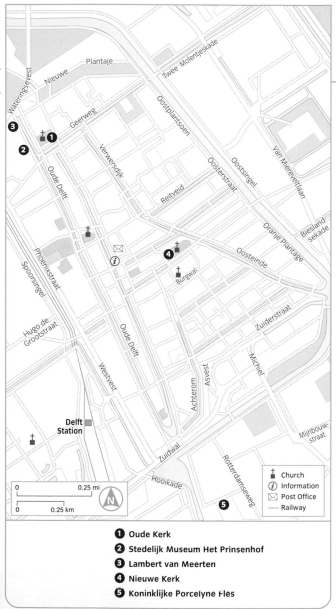

Plantaje

Twee Molentjeskade

Wateringsevest

Nieuwe

Geerweg

Oostplantsoen

Oosterstraat

Oostsingel

Van Mierevelthaan

❸

❶

❷

Oude Delft

Verwersdijk

Reitveld

Oranje Plantage

Biesland-sekade

Oosteinde

✉

ⓘ

❹

Burgwal

Phoenixstraat

Spoorsingel

Zuiderstraat

Hugo de Grootstraat

Oude Delft

Westvest

Achterom

Asvest

Michiel

Mijnbouw-straat

Delft Station

Zuidwal

Rotterdamseweg

Hooikade

❺

| | 0 | 0.25 mi |
| | 0 | 0.25 km |

N

✝ Church
ⓘ Information
✉ Post Office
— Railway

❶ Oude Kerk

❷ Stedelijk Museum Het Prinsenhof

❸ Lambert van Meerten

❹ Nieuwe Kerk

❺ Koninklijke Porcelyne Fles

Delft is best known as the home of the famous blue-and-white porcelain, and on this tour you'll visit the factory where it's produced. Delft is also a small, charming city that was the cradle of the Dutch Republic, the burial place of the royal family, and the birthplace and inspiration of artist Jan Vermeer, the 17th-century master of light and subtle emotion. Take a stroll through Delft and admire the colorful flower boxes and linden trees bending over gracious canals.

1 ★★★ Oude Kerk (Old Church). Vermeer's house is long gone from Delft, as are his paintings, but he's buried at Oude Kerk. This beautiful 13th-century church is notable for its 27 stained-glass windows. Also note the leaning clock tower built in the 14th century and the Gothic north transept, which was added in the 16th century by Belgian architect Anthonis Keldermans. The interior floors are paved with tomb slabs from the 17th century. *Roland Holstlaan 753.* ☎ *015/212-3015. Admission 3€. Open Apr–Oct Mon–Sat 9am–6pm; Nov–Mar Mon–Fri 11am–4pm, Sat 11am–5pm.*

A medieval gate.

Old Church, with its leaning clock tower.

2 ★★ Stedelijk Museum Het Prinsenhof. The "Father of the Nation," William I of Orange (William the Silent), lived and had his head-quarters here in the years when he helped found the Dutch Republic. He was also assassinated here, in 1584, and you can still see the bullet holes in the stairwell. Today the Prinsenhof is a museum of paint-ings, tapestries, silverware, and pot-tery, and is the site of the annual Delft Art and Antiques Fair, held late in October or early November. On the top floor, don't miss the accu-rately lit and detailed features of every militiaman's face in the *Civic Guard Banquet* (1611). There is also a beautiful collection of Dutch wineglasses from the 17th century. ⏱ *1 hr. Sint-Agathaplein 1.* ☎ *015/260-2358. www.prinsenhof-delft.nl. Admission 5€. Open Tues–Sat 10am–5pm; Sun & holidays 1–5pm.*

Delft Basics

Delft is only 15 minutes by train (or 25 min. by tram) from The Hague. You'll have to change trains in The Hague to get here, an easy feat, or you can combine a visit to Delft with a visit to The Hague or Rotterdam. The one-way fare from Amsterdam to Delft is 8.60€. Or you can travel just to The Hague and then jump on a tram for 2.30€ to Delft. From the Delft railway station, most everything is just a 10-minute walk. Tram 1 does the journey from The Hague to Delft two to three times an hour, depending on the day.

For information, **Tourist Information Delft,** Hippolytusbuurt 4, 2611 HN Delft (☎ **015/215-4051;** www.delft.nl), is in the center of town. The office is open Sunday and Monday from 10am to 4pm, Tuesday to Friday from 9am to 6pm, and Saturday from 9am to 5pm.

❸ ★★ Lambert van Meerten. A visit to this elaborately designed canalside home will give you a glimpse into the lives of the prosperous in Delft. Built in 1892 for a wealthy patron of the arts, Lambert van Meerten, this beautiful neo-Renaissance-style house has a fine collection of old Delft tiles displayed in the wood-paneled walls. Be sure to look up at the Delft-tile vases placed discreetly above the door-frames. Even the fireplace is adorned with blue-and-white Delft tiles. After your visit it's worth a stroll across the canal to admire the house from afar. ⏱ *45 min. Best time to come is late afternoon, when it's less crowded & the sun slanting through the back windows splashes the tiles with light. Oude Delft 199.* ☎ *015/260-2358. Admission 3.50€. Open Tues–Sat 10am–5pm; Sun & holidays 1–5pm.*

❹ ★★ Nieuwe Kerk. Prince William of Orange and other members of the House of Oranje-Nassau are buried here. The church was built between 1383 and 1510, and most of it was restored following a fire in 1536. Renowned architect PJH Cuypers added the 100m (320-ft.) tower to the Gothic facade.

Dutch architect and sculptor Hendrick de Keyser designed the ornate black-and-white marble tomb of William of Orange. After your visit to the interior, leave some time to stroll around the square, admiring the church and its spire from different angles. *Markt.* ☎ *015/212-3025. Admission 2€. Open Apr–Oct Mon–Sat 9am–6pm; Nov–Mar Mon–Fri 11am–4pm, Sat 11am–5pm.*

The interior of New Church.

You can see artists at work at Delft's Porcelain Factory.

⑤ ★★★ Koninklijke Porcelyne Fles (Porcelain Factory). If you like Delft tiles, you'll be in heaven here. Not only will you get to visit the factory and get a firsthand view of the business of painting tiles, but you can also visit the Delft museum and shop at the showroom for factory seconds at incredible bargains. But perhaps the highlight of any visit here is the 1-hour workshop that teaches you to paint your own series of tiles. The tiles are then fired and glazed and are ready for pickup after 48 hours (or they can be shipped to your home address). The workshop costs 33€ per person and includes the tiles but not the shipping and handling costs. These workshops are available from 9am to 3:30pm, and it's advisable to call ahead for reservations. *Rotterdamseweg 196.* ☎ *015/251-2030. www.royaldelft. com. Tour 2.50€; 1-hr. workshop 33€. Open Apr–Oct Mon–Sat 9am–5pm, Sun 9:30am–4pm; Nov–Mar Mon–Sat 9am–5pm.*

Rotterdam

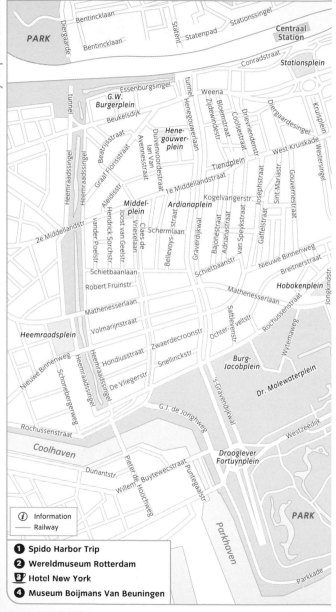

PARK

Diergaarde

Bentincklaan

Bentincklaan

Statent

Statenpad

Stationssingel

Conradstraat

Centraal Station

Stationsplein

tunnel

Essenburgsingel

Weena

G.W. Burgerplein

Beukelsdijk

Henegouwerlaan

Bloemstraat

Zijdewindestr.

Drievriendenstr.

Coolsestraat

Diergaardesingel

Kruisplein

West-Kruiskade

Westersingel

Heemraadssingel

tunnel

Beatrijsstraat

Graaf Florisstraat

Jan Van Avennesstraat

Duivenvoordestraat

Henegouwerplein

Tiendplein

1e Middellandstraat

Josephstraat

Sint-Mariastr.

Gaffelstraat

Gouvernestraat

Heemraadssingel

Aleidisstr.

Middelplein

Ardianaplein

Kogelvangerstr.

2e Middellandstr.

Hendrick Sorchstr.

Joost van Geelstr.

Claes de Vrieselaan

vander Poelstr.

Schermlaan

Bellevoysstraat

Graverdijkwal

Bajonetstraat

Adrianastraat

van Speykstraat

Nieuwe Binnenweg

Breitnerstraat

Jongkindstr.

Schietbaanlaan

Schietbaanstr.

Hobokenplein

Robert Fruinstr.

Mathenesserlaan

Mathenesserlaan

Rochussenstraat

Wytemaweg

Volmarijnstraat

Satlieveveltstr.

Ochterveltstr.

Heemraadsplein

Nieuwe Binnenweg

Schonebergerweg

Heemraadssingel

Hondiusstraat

De Vliegerstr.

Zwaerdecroonstr.

Snellinckstr.

Burg-Jacobplein

Dr. Molewaterplein

G.J. de Jonghweg

's-Gravendijkwal

Rochussenstraat

Coolhaven

Dunantstr.

Pieter de Hoochweg

Willem de Buytewecstraat

Puntegaalstr.

Drooglever Fortuynplein

Westzeedijk

PARK

Parkhaven

Parkkade

(i) Information

— Railway

❶ Spido Harbor Trip

❷ Wereldmuseum Rotterdam

❸ Hotel New York

❹ Museum Boijmans Van Beuningen

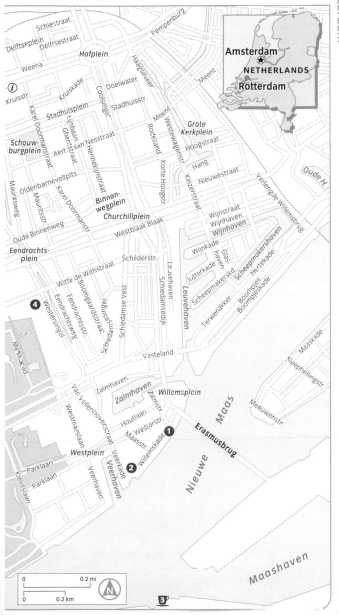

Amsterdam
NETHERLANDS
Rotterdam

ffectionately referred to as "Manhattan by the Maas" (the large river that runs through it and out to sea), Rotterdam was completely destroyed during World War II. Its vibrant newness is part of its attraction. Rotterdam also has an important place in American history: Delfshaven, one of the only areas not entirely damaged during World War II, is the port from which Dutch immigrants left to sail out to the new continent.

❶ ★★★ kids Spido Harbor Trip.

The best way to tour Rotterdam is by taking this large, comfortable boat up and down the Maas River and deep into the world's largest port. You pass under the city's most scenic landmark, the Erasmus Bridge (or Swan Bridge as it's called by the locals), and you pass Delftshaven and its old mill (from where the pilgrims left for America in 1620). You get fabulous views of the Euromast, Rotterdam's tallest structure, built in 1960. But the most fascinating aspect of this tour is its up-close-and-personal view of the workings of this immense port: You zigzag around immense cranes, tankers, barges, and all kinds of boats and ships. Older kids and anybody with a maritime interest will love this trip. ⏱ 1½ hr. Willemsplein 85 (under the Erasmus Bridge). ☎ 010/275-9988. www.spido.nl. Tickets 8.50€ adults, 5.10€ children 4–11, free for children under 4

Get an up-close look at Swan Bridge on a tour of Rotterdam's harbor.

(there's a ticket office opposite of where the boat is docked). Apr–Sept departures every 30–45 min. 9:30am–5pm; Oct–Mar usually 2–3 trips per day with the last one at

Delfshaven.

Rotterdam Basics

Trains leave Amsterdam's Centraal Station every half-hour for the 1-hour, 15-minute trip to Rotterdam. All the trains stop at Amsterdam's Schiphol Airport before continuing on to Rotterdam; some trains make an additional stop in The Hague before reaching Rotterdam, adding 5 minutes to the trip. The one-way fare is 7.40€. Once in Rotterdam, you can use the trams with the same tickets you used in Amsterdam. Taxis are plentiful, too. The Rotterdam airport, 15 minutes from the city center, is small and compact and served by several budget European airlines. Consider flying into Amsterdam and out of Rotterdam to take advantage of the compact airport's swift departure and arrival formalities.

For information, **VVV Rotterdam,** Coolsingel 67, 3012 AC Rotterdam (☎ **0900/403-4065;** fax 010/413-3124; www.vvvrotterdam. nl; Metro: Stadhuis), is on the corner of Stadhuisplein. The office is open Monday to Thursday from 9:30am to 6pm, Friday from 9:30am to 9pm, Saturday from 9:30am to 5pm, and Sunday (Apr–Sept) from noon to 5pm.

3pm; check the company's website or call ahead for winter hours. Tram: 5 to Westerplein.

❷ ★★ Wereldmuseum Rotterdam. A mere 5-minute stroll from the Spido-boat-trip dock, you'll spot this striking white building formerly known as the Museum of Ethnology. It's now the World Art Museum and holds over 200,000 items from around the world. Built in 1851, the museum boasts a large collection of 17th century objects, most picked up by Dutch sailors during the Golden Age. Indonesia figures strongly in the collection, with musical instruments, masks, and textiles, among many other objects. But that's just the tip of the iceberg. The early photographs from 1860 are worth a visit to the museum alone, and anybody interested in geography will love perusing the staggering number of antique maps and world atlases on display. The museum claims to have one of the largest collections of Australian

Aboriginal art in western Europe. The Islamic Cultural Area features artifacts from the Ottoman Empire and an amazing collection of silk textiles with gold embroidery. *Willemskade 25.* ☎ *010/270-7172. www.wereldmuseum.rotterdam.nl. Admission 6€. Tues–Sun 10am–5pm. Tram: 5 to Westerplein.*

Hotel New York

3 Hotel New York. What was once the headquarters for the Holland America shipping lines is now a modern hotel with a lovely cafe-restaurant on its ground floor. You can take a water taxi to get here (from the tiny marina at the edge of Willemskade facing the Wereldmuseum). The water taxi, small and wooden, is in itself part of the allure of the Hotel New York. It costs 2€ each way. Once here, settle into a waterside table and enjoy large American-style salads (like Chef's or Caesar) or order some samples from the wonderful oyster bar. If there are strong winds, the water taxi will not operate and you can just hail a normal cab that will drive you the to the left bank over the Erasmus bridge (a 5-min. trip). *Koninginnenhoofd 1.* ☎ *010/439-0500. www.hotelnewyork.nl. $$.*

4 Museum Boijmans Van Beuningen. Hail a cab or take the tram to yet another of Holland's treasure troves of fine art. Here, you'll find walls and walls of paintings by the Dutch masters as well as works by Degas, Dali, Man Ray, and Tintoretto. There's a fine collection of porcelain, silver, glass, and delftware, too. Don't miss Rembrandt's lovely *Titus at his Desk* (1655), which depicts his son deep in thought with the gentlest play of light and shadow to portray a slightly brooding mood. Among the many beautiful objects from the 17th century is a 215-centimeter (7-ft.) clock made of walnut wood that will take your breath away. When you're done, you can take a 15-minute walk back to the railway station or catch the tram or a taxi. *Museumpark 18–20.* ☎ *010/441-9400. www. boijmans.rotterdam.nl. Admission 7€. Open Tues–Sat 10am–5pm; Sun & holidays 11am–5pm. Tram: 5 to Museumpark.* ●

A Grand Harbor

A dredged deep-water channel connects Rotterdam with the North Sea and forms a 32km-long (20-mile) harbor known as **Europoort** (*"poort"* is pronounced like "port" in English). This handles more ships and more cargo every year than any other port in the world—20,000 ships and 310 million metric tons of cargo. You may think visiting a harbor is boring business on a vacation, but Rotterdam's is one of the most memorable sights in Holland and makes any other harbor you've ever seen look like a Fisher-Price toy.

Container ships, bulk carriers, tankers, sleek greyhounds of the sea, and careworn tramps are waited on by a vast retinue of machines and people. Trucks, trains, and barges, each carrying its little piece of the action, hurry into and out from the hub. Europoort is the pump that replenishes Europe's commercial arteries.

The **Savvy Traveler**

Before You Go

Government Tourist Offices

FOR THE U.S. & CANADA: Netherlands Board of Tourism (NBT), 355 Lexington Ave., 19th Floor, New York, NY 10017 (☎ 888/464-6552 or 212/557-3500; fax 212/370-9507; www.visit holland.com). **FOR THE U.K. & IRELAND:** No phone or walk-in service. NBT, PO Box 30783, London WC2B 6DH. Premium-rate brochure order line ☎ 09068/717-777 (www.visit holland.com/uk; information@nbt. org.uk). **IN HOLLAND:** NBT, Vlietweg 15, Postbus 458, 2260 MG Leidschendam (☎ 31-70/371-5705; fax 31-70/320-1654; info@nbt.nl).

The Best Times to Go

In-season in Amsterdam means from mid-April to mid-October. The peak of the tourist season is July and August, when the weather is at its finest. Weather, however, is never really extreme at any time of year; and if you're one of the growing numbers who favor shoulder- or off-season travel, you'll find the city every bit as attractive. Not only are airlines, hotels, and restaurants cheaper and less crowded during the off season (with more relaxed and personalized service), but there are also some very appealing events going on. You may want to go when the bulb fields near Amsterdam are bursting with color from mid-April to mid-May, one of the best times to visit Holland.

Festivals & Special Events

SPRING. Late March to mid-May, catch the **OPENING OF KEUKENHOF GARDENS,** Lisse. The greatest flower show on earth blooms with a spectacular display of tulips, narcissi, daffodils, hyacinths, bluebells, crocuses, lilies, amaryllis, and many other flowers at this 28-hectare (70-acre) garden in the heart of the bulb country. There's said to be nearly eight million flowers, but who's counting? Contact **KEUKENHOF** (☎ 025/246-5555).

During **NATIONAL MUSEUM WEEKEND** (the second weekend in Apr), most museums in Amsterdam and many throughout the Netherlands offer free or reduced admission and have special exhibits.

On April 30 all of Holland celebrates **KONINGINNEDAG (QUEEN'S DAY)** with a gigantic dawn-to-dawn street carnival. The city center gets so jam-packed with people that it's virtually impossible to move. A citywide street market features masses of stalls. Orange ribbons, orange hair, and orange-painted faces are everywhere, as are Dutch flags. Street music and theater combine with lots of drinking during this good-natured if boisterous affair. *Tip:* Wear something orange, even if it's only an orange cap or an orange ribbon in your hair. Contact **VVV AMSTERDAM** (☎ 0900/400-4040) for more information.

The second Saturday in May is **NATIONAL WINDMILL DAY** throughout Holland. Around two-thirds of the country's almost 1,000 windmills spin their sails and are open to the public, including Amsterdam's eight. Contact **VERENIGING DE HOLLANDSE MOLEN** (☎ 020/623-8703).

During the last 2 weeks in May, **FLOATING AMSTERDAM** transforms the lower reaches of the Amstel River into an outdoor theater. Performances are held near the Muziektheater. Contact **VVV AMSTERDAM** (☎ 0900/400-4040) or **AMSTERDAM UIT BURO** (☎ 0900/0191).

You can either watch or join in during **ECHO GRACHTENLOOP (ECHO**

CANAL RUN), the last Sunday in May or first Sunday in June.

Thousands of footloose people run along the city center canals on 5km, 10km, and 18km routes (3, 6, and 11 miles). Contact **ECHO GRACHT-ENLOOP** (☎ 020/585-9222).

SUMMER. From June to mid-August, catch a performance at the **VONDEL-PARK OPEN-AIR THEATER.** Everything goes here: theater, all kinds of music (including full-scale classical concerts by the famed Concertgebouw Orchestra), dance, and even operettas. Contact **VONDELPARK OPENLUCHTTHEATER** (☎ 020/673-1499).

In late June you can see **CANAL-HOUSE GARDENS IN BLOOM** on Herengracht, Keizersgracht, and Prinsengracht. If you wonder what the gardens behind the gables of all those fancy canalside houses look like, this is your chance to find out. A number of the best are open to the public for 3 days. Contact **STICHTING DE AMSTERDAMSE GRACHT-ENTUIN** (☎ 020/422-2379).

Europe's most gay-friendly city hosts the **AMSTERDAM PRIDE** event in early August. A crowd of 150,000 people turns out to watch the Boat Parade, in which some 100 outrageously decorated boats cruise the canals. In addition, there are street discos, open-air theater performances, a sports program, and a film festival. (The entire festival's future is in the balance: The City Council is considering revoking permission for the festival on "public order" grounds.) Contact **GAY BUSINESS AMSTERDAM** (☎/fax 020/620-8807).

FALL. During **OPEN MONUMENTENDAG,** on the second Saturday in September, you have a chance to see historical buildings and monuments that are usually not open to the public—and to get in free as well. Contact **VERENIGING OPEN MONUMENTENDAG** (☎ 020/470-1170).

Participants in the most popular running event in the country, **DAM TO DAMLOOP (DAM TO DAM RUN),** start at the Dam in the center of Amsterdam, head out of town through the IJ Tunnel to the center of Zaandam, and return to the Dam, for a distance of 16km (10 miles). Contact **DAM TO DAMLOOP** (☎ 072/533-8136; www.damloop.nl). It takes place the third Sunday in September, starting at noon.

Queen Beatrix rides in a splendid gold coach to the Ridderzaal (Knights' Hall) in The Hague for the **STATE OPENING OF PARLIAMENT,** which opens the legislative session. Contact **VVV DEN HAAG** (☎ 0900/340-5051). Third Tuesday in September.

SINTERKLAAS, Holland's equivalent of Santa Claus (St. Nicholas) launches the Christmas season when he arrives in the city by boat at the Centraal Station pier. Accompanied by black-painted assistants called *Zwarte Piet* (Black Peter) who hand out sweets to kids along the way, he goes in stately procession through Amsterdam before being given the keys to the city by the mayor at the Dam. Contact **VVV AMSTERDAM** (☎ 0900/400-4040). Third Saturday of November.

WINTER. The city's **NEW YEAR'S** celebrations take place throughout the center, but mostly at the Dam and Nieuwmarkt. Things get wild and not always so wonderful. Many of Amsterdam's youthful spirits celebrate the new year with firecrackers, which they throw at the feet of passersby. This keeps hospital emergency departments busy. January 1.

More than 300 indie films are screened at theaters around town during the **ROTTERDAM INTERNATIONAL FILM FESTIVAL,** from late January to early February. Contact (☎ 010/411-8080; www.filmfestival rotterdam.com).

AMSTERDAM'S AVERAGE MONTHLY TEMPERATURES

	JAN	FEB	MAR	APR	MAY	JUNE	JULY	AUG	SEPT	OCT	NOV	DEC
Temp. (°F)	36	36	41	46	54	59	62	62	58	51	44	38
Temp. (°C)	2	2	5	8	12	15	17	17	14	11	7	3

During **CARNIVAL**, Amsterdammers attempt to show that they can party just as wildly as their southern compatriots at *their* carnivals in Maastricht and Den Bosch. An objective observer (one who's still sober) would have to report that the Amsterdammers fail miserably, mainly because the southerners are the true Dutch experts on the art of carnival. Still, Amsterdam's carnival will give you a taste of what it's all about if you can't make it to one of the southern ones. Contact **VVV AMSTERDAM** (☎ *0900/400-4040*). Early February.

The Weather

Summers are warm and pleasant, with only a few oppressively hot days. However, air-conditioned hotels are rare, so those few days can be quite uncomfortable. Rain is common throughout the year, especially in winter.

Useful Websites

- www.visitholland.com and www.visitamsterdam.com offer comprehensive information, covering hotels, sightseeing, and notices of special events.

- www.amsterdamhotspots.nl lists the latest places to see and be seen in the city.

- www.hollandmuseums.nl is loaded with information about the city's museums—more than 40 of them.

Cell (Mobile) Phones

If your phone has GSM (Global System for Mobiles) capability and you have a world-compatible phone, you should be able to make and receive calls from Holland. Only certain phones have this capability, though, and you should check with your service operator first. Call charges can be high. Alternatively, you can rent a phone through **CELLHIRE** (www.cellhire.com; www.cellhire.co.uk; www.cellhire.com.au). After a simple online registration, they will ship a phone (usually with a U.K. number) to your home or office. Usage charges can be astronomical, so read the fine print.

U.K. mobiles work in Holland; call your service provider before departing your home country to ensure that the international call bar has been switched off and to check call charges, which can be extremely high. Also remember that you are charged for calls you *receive* on a U.K. mobile used abroad.

Car Rentals

There's very little need to rent a car in Amsterdam, but if you're determined to do so, it's usually cheapest to book a car online before you leave home. Try **HERTZ** (www.hertz.com), **AVIS** (www.avis.com), or **BUDGET** (www.budget.com). You should also consider **AUTOEUROPE** (www.autoeurope.com), which sends you a prepaid voucher, locking in the exchange rate.

Getting **There**

By Plane

ARRIVING: AMSTERDAM AIRPORT
SCHIPHOL (☎ *0900/0141* for general and flight information; www. schiphol.nl), 13km (8 miles) southwest of the city center, is the main airport in the Netherlands, handling just about all of the country's international arrivals and departures. Frequent travelers regularly vote Schiphol (pronounced *Skhip-*ol) one of the world's favorite airports for its ease of use and its massive, duty-free shopping center.

After you deplane at one of the three terminals (all close together and numbered 1, 2, and 3), moving walkways take you to the Arrivals Hall, where you pass through Passport Control, Customs, and Baggage Reclaim. Conveniences like free luggage carts, currency exchange, ATMs, restaurants, bars, shops, baby-rooms, restrooms, and showers are available. Beyond these is Schiphol Plaza, which combines rail station access, the Airport Hotel, a mall (sporting that most essential Dutch service—a flower store), bars and restaurants, restrooms, baggage lockers, airport and tourist information desks, car-rental and hotel reservation desks, and more, all in a single location. Bus, shuttle, and taxi stops are just outside.

For tourist information and to make hotel reservations, go to the **HOLLAND TOURIST INFORMATION (HTI)** desk in Schiphol Plaza (☎ *0900/400-4040*), open daily from 7am to 10pm.

GETTING INTO TOWN: Netherlands Railways **TRAINS** for Amsterdam Centraal Station depart from Schiphol Station, downstairs from Schiphol Plaza, and stop at De Lelylaan and De Vlugtlaan stations in west Amsterdam on the way. Frequency ranges from six trains an hour at peak times to one an hour at night. The fare is 2.95€ one-way; the trip takes 20 minutes.

An alternative rail route serves both Amsterdam Zuid/WTC (World Trade Center) station and RAI station (beside the big RAI Convention Center). If you're staying at a hotel near Leidseplein, Rembrandtplein, in the Museum Quarter, or in Amsterdam South, this route may be a better bet for you than Centraal Station. The fare is 2.95€ one-way; the trip takes around 15 minutes. From Amsterdam Zuid/WTC, take tram no. 5 for Leidseplein and the Museum Quarter; from RAI, take tram no. 4 for Rembrandtplein.

The **CONNEXXION HOTEL BUS** (☎ *0900/9292*) shuttles between the airport and Amsterdam, serving 16 top hotels directly and many more that are close to these stops. The fare is 8.50€ one-way (13€ round-trip) to the contracted hotels, or 11€ one-way (19€ round-trip) to noncontracted hotels. No reservations are needed and buses depart from in front of Schiphol Plaza every 20 minutes from 7am to 5pm, every 30 minutes from 5 to 7pm, and every hour from 7 to 9pm. If you're not staying at one of the contracted hotels, the clerks from the Connexxion Desk inside Schiphol Plaza can tell you which shuttle stop is closest to your chosen lodgings. The bus takes anywhere from 40 minutes to 1½ hours.

BUS no. 197 departs every half-hour from in front of Schiphol Plaza for Amsterdam's downtown Marnixstraat bus station. Line 199 serves the Amstel railway station in Amsterdam South. Buses depart every 30 minutes at peak time and every hour at other times. The fare on both buses is 3.40€. These buses are a lot slower than both the train and the Connexxion Hotel Bus—the trip takes about 1 hour and 15 minutes.

You'll find **TAXIS** waiting at the stands of **SCHIPHOLTAXI** (☎ 020/653-1000; www.schipoltaxi.nl) in front of Schiphol Plaza. Taxis from the airport are all metered. Expect to pay around 48€ to the city center; the trip takes 35 to 45 minutes. A service charge is already included in the fare.

By Boat from Britain

DFDS SEAWAYS (☎ 08705/333111 in Britain; 0255/534-546 in Holland; www.dfdsseaways.co.uk) has daily car-ferry service between Newcastle in northeast England and IJmuiden on the North Sea coast west of Amsterdam. The overnight trip time is 15 hours. From IJmuiden, you can either go by train to Amsterdam Centraal Station or by jet-foil with **FAST FLYING FERRIES** (☎ 020/423-0805) to a pier behind Centraal Station.

P&O FERRIES (☎ 08705/202020 Britain; 0181/255-555 Holland; www.poferries.com) has daily car-ferry service between Hull in northeast England and Rotterdam (Europoort). The overnight trip time is 10 hours. Ferry-company coaches shuttle passengers between the Rotterdam Europoort terminal and Rotterdam Centraal Station, from where there are frequent trains to Amsterdam.

STENA LINE (☎ 08705/707070 Britain; 0174/389-333 Holland; www.stenaline.com) has fast, twice-daily car-ferry service between Harwich in southeast England and Hoek van Holland (Hook of Holland) near Rotterdam. The trip time is 3 hours, 40 minutes. Frequent trains depart from Hoek van Holland to Rotterdam and Amsterdam.

By Cruise Ship

Cruise-ship passengers arrive in Amsterdam at the **PASSENGER TERMINAL AMSTERDAM,** Oostelijke Handelskade 9 (☎ 020/418-6854; www.ptamsterdam.com; IJ-tram), on the IJ waterway within easy walking distance of Centraal Station.

By Train

Rail service to Amsterdam from other cities in the Netherlands and elsewhere in Europe is frequent and fast. International and Intercity express trains arrive at Centraal Station from Brussels and Paris, from several German cities, and from more distant locations in eastern Europe, Spain, Austria, Switzerland, and Italy. There's also an Intercity train between Amsterdam and Brussels. Connections can be made in Brussels to the North Express, the Oostende-Vienna Express, the Oostende-Moscow Express, and the Trans-Europe Express. **NEDERLANDSE SPOORWEGEN** (Netherlands Railways; www.ns.nl) trains arrive in Amsterdam from towns and cities all over Holland. Service is frequent to many places around the country and trains are modern, clean, and punctual. Schedule and fare information on travel by train and other public transportation *(openbaar vervoer)* in the Netherlands is available from ☎ 0900/9292, or visit *www.9292ov.nl*; for international trains, call ☎ 0900/9296.

The distinctive burgundy-colored **THALYS** (www.thalys.com) high-speed train, with a top speed of 300kmph (186 mph), connecting Paris, Brussels, Amsterdam, and (via Brussels) Cologne, has cut travel times from Paris to Amsterdam to 4¼ hours, and from Brussels to 2¼ hours—figures that will be reduced to closer to 3¼ hours and 1¾ hours, respectively, when the high-speed rail lines in Holland are operational.

For Thalys information and reservations in France, call ☎ 08/3635-3536; in Belgium, ☎ 0800/95-777; in Germany, ☎ 0221/19419; and in Holland, ☎ 0900/9296. Tickets are also available from many railway stations and travel agents. On the **EUROSTAR** (www.eurostar.com) high-speed train (top speed 258kmph/160 mph), the travel time between London Waterloo Station and Brussels Midi Station (the closest connecting point for Amsterdam) is 3¼ hours. On weekends the respective one-way fares are approximately £140 from London to Brussels, and £100 from Brussels to Amsterdam. Departures from London to Brussels are approximately every 2 hours at peak times. For Eurostar reservations, call ☎ 08701/606600 in Britain or ☎ 020/423-4444 in Holland.

ARRIVING AT CENTRAAL STATION: Regardless of where they originate, most visitors traveling to Amsterdam by train find themselves deposited at Amsterdam's Centraal Station, built from 1884–89 on an artificial island in the IJ channel. The building, an ornate architectural wonder on its own, is the focus of much activity. It's at the hub of the city's concentric rings of canals and connecting main streets, and is the originating point for most of the city's trams, Metro trains, and buses.

You'll find an office of VVV Amsterdam tourist information inside the station on platform 2 and another office right in front of the station on Stationsplein; both offices have hotel reservation desks. Other facilities include a GWK Bureau de Change, ATMs, a train info center, luggage lockers, restaurants and snack bars, newsstands, and some small specialty stores.

WARNING: Centraal Station is home to a pickpocket convention that's in full swing at all times. Messages broadcast in multiple languages warn people to be on their guard, but the artful dodgers still seem to do good business. Avoid becoming one of their victims by keeping your money and other valuables under wraps, especially among crowds. You're also likely to notice a heroin addict or two, a platoon of panhandlers, and more than a whiff of pot smoke in the air.

An array of tram stops are on either side of the main station exit—virtually all of Amsterdam's hotels are within a 15-minute tram ride from Centraal Station. The Metro station is downstairs, just outside the main exit. City bus stops are to the left of the main exit, and the taxi stands are to the right. At the public transportation Tickets & Info office on Stationsplein, you can buy a *strippenkaart* or *dagkaart* for trams, Metros, and buses (see "Getting Around," below, for more information). The station is also a departure point for passenger ferries across the IJ waterway and around the harbor, water taxis, canal-boat tours, the Museum Boat, and the Canal Bus.

By Bus

International coaches—and in particular those of **EUROLINES** (www.eurolines.com)—arrive at the bus terminal opposite the Amstel rail station (Metro: Amstel) in the south of the city. **EUROLINES** operates coach service between London Victoria Bus Station and Amstel Station (via ferry), with up to five departures daily in the summer. Travel time is just over 12 hours. For reservations, contact Eurolines (☎ 08705/808080 in Britain or 020/560-8788 in Holland). From here you can go by train and Metro train to Centraal Station, and by tram no. 12 to the Museumplein area and to connecting points for trams to the city center. For the Leidseplein area, take the Metro toward Centraal Station, get out at Weesperplein, and go aboveground to take tram line 6, 7, or 10.

By Car

A network of major international highways crisscrosses Holland. European expressways E19, E35, E231, and E22 converge on Amsterdam from France and Belgium to the south and from Germany to the north and east. These roads also have Dutch designations; as you approach the city they are, respectively: A4, A2, A1, and A7. Amsterdam's ring road is A10. Distances between destinations are relatively short. Traffic is invariably heavy, but road conditions are otherwise excellent, service stations are plentiful, and highways are plainly signposted.

Getting **Around**

By Public Transportation

Visitors intending to make frequent use of Amsterdam's public transportation options should consider purchasing the **ALL AMSTERDAM TRANSPORT PASS,** valid on the Canal Bus, trams, buses, and the Metro. It's 17€ a day and is available from GVB Tickets & Info, VVV tourist information offices, the Canal Bus company. It's a good value if you make extensive use of its unlimited travel facility on both the Canal Bus and GVB public transportation.

The weirdly named nationale strippenkaart (national strip card) is the best way to travel in Amsterdam because it allows you to "strip" off the number of tickets you need for the different zones in the city and its suburbs. The tickets can be used on any tram, bus, and Metro not only in Amsterdam but in all of Holland's cities—so if you're going to the Hague or Rotterdam, you can use your strippenkaarts there, too. Strippenkaarts with 8 tickets cost 12€, 15 tickets cost 11.75€, and 45 tickets cost 33.50€. You can purchase strippenkaarts at Metro stations and at the tram office facing Centraal Station. You can also buy tram, bus, and Metro tickets individually, either at Metro stations or on the tram or bus. Individual tickets cost 1.50€ to 3€, depending on the zones you are traveling from and to.

BY TRAM: Half the fun of Amsterdam is walking along the canals. The other half is riding the smooth blue-and-light-gray trams that roll through most major streets. There are 16 tram routes, 11 of which (lines 1, 2, 4, 5, 6, 9, 13, 16, 17, 24, and 25) begin and end at Centraal Station, so you know you can always get back to that central point if you get lost and have to start over. The other tram routes are 3, 7, 10, 12, and 14.

Most trams have conductors, and on these the only available access door opens automatically; you board toward the rear (in the case of the oldest trams, at the rear) following arrowed indicators that point the way to the door. To board a tram that has no such arrowed indicators (and no conductor), push the button on the outside of the car beside any door. Getting off, you may need to push a button with an "open-door" graphic or the words *deur open.* Tram doors close automatically, and they do it quite quickly, so don't hang around.

BY BUS: An extensive bus network complements the trams. Many bus routes begin and end at Centraal Station. It's generally faster to go by tram if you have the option, but some points in the city are served only by bus.

BY METRO: It can't compare to the labyrinthine systems of Paris, London, and New York, but Amsterdam does have its own Metro, with four lines—50, 51, 53, and 54—that run partly overground and bring people in from the suburbs and home again. You may want to take them simply as a sightseeing excursion, though to be frank, few of the sights on the lines are worth going out of your way for. On these lines you validate your strip card on the platform before boarding.

A new Metro line, the Metro Noord/Zuidlijn, is currently under construction to link Amsterdam Noord, under the IJ, then south through the city center all the way to Station Zuid/WTC. It's due to be completed in 2011.

BY FERRY: FREE FERRIES for passengers and two-wheel transportation connect the city center with Amsterdam Noord (North), across the IJ channel. The short crossings are free, which makes them ideal microcruises for the cash-strapped, and they afford fine views of the harbor. Sadly, there's little of interest in Noord, so the free trip may have to be its own attraction. Ferries depart from piers along De Ruyterkade behind Centraal Station. One route connects Pier 7 and Buiksloterweg on the north shore, with ferries every 10 to 15 minutes. A second route connects Pier 8 and IJplein, a more easterly point on the north shore, with ferries every 10 to 15 minutes. Both services operate round the clock.

A third service, for which you pay 1.30€, departs every half-hour or so from Pier 8 to Java Island in the Eastern Docks, and across the several points on the north shore (a half-hour trip that provides a more satisfactory view of the harbor). Exact routing varies.

BY WATER BUS: Two different companies operate water buses (rarely, if ever, used by locals) that bring you to, or close to, many of the city's museums, attractions, and shopping and entertainment districts. **CANAL BUS** (020/623-9886; www.canal.nl) has three routes—Green Line, Red Line, and Blue Line—with stops that include Centraal Station, Westermarkt, Leidseplein, Rijksmuseum (with an extension to the RAI Convention Center when big shows are on there), Waterlooplein, and East Amsterdam. Hours of operation are daily from 10am to 6:30pm, with two buses an hour at peak times. A day pass, valid until noon the next day and including a discount on some museum and attraction admissions, is 14€ for adults, 11€ for children ages 3 to 12, and free for children under 3.

The **MUSEUMBOOT** (020/530-1090; www.lovers.nl)—pronounced "museum boat"—transports weary tourists on their pilgrimages from museum to museum and has the added benefit of providing some of the features of a canal-boat cruise. Boats depart from the Rederij Lovers dock in front of Centraal Station daily from 10am to 5pm, every 30 minutes in summer, and every 45 minutes in winter. They stop at seven key spots, providing access to museums and other sights. These include the Rijksmuseum, Van Gogh Museum, Stedelijk Museum, Anne Frankhuis, Leidseplein, Vondelpark, Amsterdams Historisch Museum, Flower Market, Museum Het Rembrandthuis, Jewish Historical Museum, Artis Zoo, Muziekthcater, Tropenmuseum, and Maritime Museum. A day ticket is 14€ for adults, 9.50€ for children ages 4 to 12, and free for children under 4; after 1pm tickets are, respectively, 13€ and 7.25€. Tickets include discounted admission to some museums and attractions.

By Taxi

It used to be that you couldn't simply hail a cab from the street in Amsterdam, but nowadays they often stop if you do. Otherwise, find one of the taxi stands sprinkled around the city, generally near the luxury hotels or at major squares such as the Dam, Stationsplein, Spui, Rembrandtplein, Westermarkt, and Leidseplein. Taxis have rooftop signs and blue license tags, and are metered.

For a generally reliable service, call **TAXI CENTRALE AMSTERDAM** (☎ 020/677-7777). TCA's fares begin at 2.90€ when the meter starts and run up at 1.80€ a kilometer, and after 25km, 1.30€ a kilometer; waiting time is 32€ per hour. The fare includes a tip, but you may round up or give something for an extra service, like help with your luggage, or for a friendly discourse.

By Water Taxi

Since you're in the city of canals, you might like to splurge on a water taxi. These launches do more or less the same thing as landlubber taxis, except that they do it on the canals and the Amstel River and in the harbor. You can move faster than on land and you get your very own canal cruise. To order one, call **WATERTAXI** (☎ 020/535-6363), or pick one up from the dock outside Centraal Station, close to the VVV office. For up to eight people the fare is 60€ for 30 minutes, plus an additional 25€ if they need to collect you.

By Bike

Instead of renting a car, follow the Dutch example and ride a bicycle. Sunday, when the city is quiet, is a particularly good day to pedal through Vondelpark and along off-the-beaten-path canals, or to practice riding on cobblestones and bike lanes, crossing bridges, and dodging trams before venturing forth into the fray of an Amsterdam rush hour.

There are more than half a million bikes in the city, so you'll have plenty of company.

Navigating the city on two wheels is mostly safe—or at any rate not as suicidal as it looks—thanks to a vast network of dedicated bike lanes. Bikes even have their own traffic lights. Amsterdam's battle-scarred bike-borne veterans make it almost a point of principle to ignore every safety rule ever written. Though they mostly live to tell the tale, don't think the same will necessarily apply for you.

Bike-rental rates are around 7€ a day or 30€ a week; a deposit is required. **MIKE'S BIKE TOURS,** Kerkstraat 134 (☎ 020/622-7970; www.mikesbiketours.com; tram: 1, 2, or 5), is a good bet for a rental. So is **MACBIKE,** which rents a range of bikes, including tandems and six-speed touring bikes. Rental outlets are at either side of Centraal Station, at Stationsplein 12 (☎ 020/624-8391) and Stationsplein 33 (☎ 020/625-3845), and at Mr. Visserplein 2 (☎ 020/620-0985; tram: 9 or 14), and Weteringschans 2 (☎ 020/528-7688; tram: 1, 2, 5, 6, 7, or 10).

WARNING: Always lock both your bike frame and one of the wheels to something solid and fixed, because theft is common.

By Car

Driving in Amsterdam is not recommended. Parking is difficult, traffic is dense, and networks of one-way streets make navigation, even with the best of maps, a problem. You would be much better advised to make use of the extensive public transport system or to take cabs.

By Foot

The best way to take in the city is to walk, and the center is very pedestrian-friendly. Carry a good map with you, and watch out for those ubiquitous speeding bikes and silent trams.

Fast **Facts**

ATMS/CASHPOINTS The easiest and best way to get cash abroad is through an ATM—the **CIRRUS** and **PLUS** networks span the globe. Most banks charge a fee for international withdrawals—check with your bank before you leave home, and find out your daily limit.

BABYSITTERS A reliable local organization is **OPPASCENTRALE KRITERION** (☎ *020/624/5848*), which has vetted babysitters over 18. Its rates are 5€ to 6€ an hour.

BANKS Most banks are open Monday to Friday from 9am to 4:30pm. A few are open on Saturday. Shops and most hotels will cash traveler's checks but not at the advantageous rate most banks and foreign exchanges will give you.

BIKE RENTALS **MACBIKE** rents a range of bikes, including tandems and six-speed touring bikes. The most convenient outlet is at Centraal Station, at Stationsplein 12 (☎ *020/624-8391*).

BUSINESS HOURS Shops tend to be open from 9:30am to 6pm. Some stay open until 8 or 9pm. Most museums close 1 day a week (often Tues), but are open most holidays except Christmas and New Year's Day.

CONSULATES & EMBASSIES **U.S. CONSULATE:** Museumplein 19 (☎ *020/575-5309*; tram: 3, 5, 12, or 16). **U.K. CONSULATE:** Koningslaan 44 (☎ *020/676-4343*; tram: 2).

Embassies are in The Hague (Den Haag): **U.S. EMBASSY,** Lange Voorhout 102 (☎ *070/310-9209*); **CANADIAN EMBASSY,** Sophialaan 7 (☎ *070/311-1600*); **U.K. EMBASSY,** Lange Voorhout 10 (☎ *070/427-0427*); **IRISH EMBASSY,** Dr. Kuyperstraat 9 (☎ *070/363-0993*); **AUSTRALIAN EMBASSY,** Carnegielaan 4 (☎ *070/310-8200*); **NEW ZEALAND EMBASSY,** Carnegielaan 10 (☎ *070/346-9324*).

CREDIT CARDS Credit cards are a safe way to carry money. They also provide a convenient record of all your expenses, and they generally offer good exchange rates. You can also withdraw cash advances from your credit cards at banks or ATMs (Cashpoints), provided you know your PIN (call the number on the back of your card if you don't know yours). Keep in mind that when you use your credit card abroad, most banks assess a 2% fee above the 1% fee charged by Visa, MasterCard, or American Express. You also pay interest from the day of your withdrawal, even if you pay your monthly bill on time.

CURRENCY EXCHANGE Cash your traveler's checks at banks or foreign-exchange offices, not at shops or hotels. Most post offices also change traveler's checks or convert money. Currency exchanges are also found at Amsterdam's airport and train stations.

CUSTOMS **NON-E.U. CITIZENS** can bring in, duty-free, 200 cigarettes, 50 cigars, 2 liters of wine, and either 1 liter of alcohol over 22 proof or 2 liters under 22 proof. Customs officials tend to be lenient about general merchandise, realizing the limits are unrealistically low. **E.U. CITIZENS** can bring any amount of goods into the Netherlands, so long as they are intended for personal use—not for resale.

DENTISTS See "Emergencies," below.

DOCTORS See "Emergencies," below.

DRUGSTORES In the Netherlands a pharmacy is called an *apotheek* and sells both prescription and nonprescription medicines. Regular open hours are Monday to Saturday from 9am to 5:30pm. A centrally located pharmacy is **DAM APOTHEEK,** Damstraat 2 (☎ 020/624-4331; tram: 4, 9, 14, 16, 24, or 25), close to the National Monument on the Dam. Pharmacies post details of nearby all-night and Sunday pharmacies on their doors.

EMERGENCIES For any emergency (fire, police, ambulance) the number is ☎ 112 from any land line or cellphone. For 24-hour emergency medical and dental service, call the **CENTRAL MEDICAL SERVICE** (☎ 020/592-3434). **U.K. NATIONALS** must have a completed and validated E111 form to receive full health benefits in the Netherlands. The system for these recently changed. Starting in 2005, you need to apply for a new form. From January 1, 2006, visitors will need the European Health Insurance Card to receive free treatment. For advice, ask at your local post office or see www.dh.gov.uk/travellers.

EVENT LISTINGS DAY BY DAY AM-STERDAM is published monthly in English and lists all the happenings around town. It's available at any newsstand for 1.75€.

FAMILY TRAVEL FAMILY TRAVEL (www.familytravel.com) is an independent, U.S.-based website offering reviews, sightseeing suggestions, and so on.

GAY & LESBIAN TRAVELERS COC, Rozenstraat 14 (☎ 020/626-3087; www.cocamsterdam.nl) is the Amsterdam branch of the Dutch lesbian and gay organization. They can answer any questions about anything gay in Holland. The city's largest gay and lesbian bookstore is **BOEKHANDEL VROLIJK,** Paleisstraat 135 (☎ 020/623-5142).

HOLIDAYS Public holidays include New Year's Day (Jan 1), Good Friday and Easter Monday (Mar or Apr), Queen's Birthday (Apr 30), Ascension Day (40 days after Easter), Pentecost Sunday (seventh Sun after Easter) and Pentecost Monday, Christmas Day (Dec 25), and Dec 26.

INSURANCE North Americans with homeowner's or renter's insurance are probably covered for lost luggage. If not, inquire with **TRAVEL ASSISTANCE INTERNATIONAL** (☎ 800/821-2828) or **TRAVELEX** (☎ 800/228-9792), insurers that can also provide trip-cancellation, medical, and emergency evacuation coverage abroad. The website www.moneysupermarket.com compares prices across a wide range of providers for single- and multitrip policies. **FOR U.K. CITIZENS,** insurance is always advisable, even if you have form E111 (see "Emergencies," above).

INTERNET ACCESS Some of the more expensive hotels offer Internet access; alternatively, to surf the Net or check your e-mail, the best place is **EASYEVERYTHING** (www.easyeverything.com) at Damrak 33 (☎ 020/320-8082; tram: 1, 2, 4, 5, 9, 13, 16, 17, 24, or 25); and Reguliersbreestraat 22 (☎ 020/320-6291; tram: 4, 9, or 14). Both are open 24 hours a day and access begins at 2€ an hour. A less-crowded choice, in a traditional Amsterdam bar that also has some computers, is the **INTERNET CAFÉ,** Martelaarsgracht 11 (☎ 020/627-1052; www.internetcafe.nl; tram: 1, 2, 5, 6, 13, or 17). It's open Sunday to Thursday from 9am to 1am and Friday and Saturday from 9am to 3am; access is 2€ an hour.

LIQUOR LAWS Supermarkets, grocery stores, and cafes sell alcoholic beverages. The legal drinking age is 16, but children under that age can be served alcohol in a bar or restaurant if accompanied by a parent or legal guardian.

LOST PROPERTY If your luggage is lost, immediately file a lost-luggage claim at the airport, detailing the luggage contents. For most airlines, you must report delayed, damaged, or lost baggage within 4 hours of arrival.

MAIL/POST OFFICES Most post offices in Amsterdam are open Monday through Friday from 9am to 5pm. Stamps can usually be purchased from your hotel reception desk and at larger newsstands, especially ones that sell postcards.

MONEY The currency of the Netherlands is the euro, which can also be used in most other E.U. countries. The exchange rate varies, but at press time, 1 euro was equal to US$1.30 and 70p in Great Britain. The best way to get cash in Amsterdam is at ATMs or Cashpoints (see above). Credit cards are accepted at almost all shops, restaurants, and hotels, but you should always have some cash on hand for incidentals and sightseeing admissions.

NEWSPAPERS & MAGAZINES Most kiosks sell English-language newspapers, including the *International Herald Tribune, USA Today,* and British titles such as the *Times* and the *Independent*.

PASSPORTS If your passport is lost or stolen, contact your country's embassy or consulate immediately (see "Consulates & Embassies," above). Before you travel, you should copy the critical pages and keep them separately from your passport itself.

POLICE Call ☎ *112* for emergencies. The most central police station is at Lijnbaansgracht 219 (☎ 0900/8844; tram 1, 2, 5, 6, 7, or 10), just off Leidseplein.

SAFETY Be especially aware of child pickpockets. Their method is to get very close to a target, ask for a handout, and deftly help themselves to your money or passport. Robbery at gun- or knifepoint is very rare but not unknown. For more information, consult the U.S. State Department's website at www.travel.state.gov; in the U.K., consult the Foreign Office's website, www.fco.gov.uk; and in Australia, consult the government

travel advisory service at www.smartraveller.gov.au.

SENIOR TRAVELERS Mention that you're a senior when you make your travel reservations. As in most cities, people over the age of 60 qualify for reduced admission to Amsterdam theaters, museums, and other attractions, as well as discounted fares on public transport.

SMOKING Smoking is common in Holland, but authorities are clamping down heavily on smoking in public places, and it's now banned in such places as theaters and on public transport.

TAXES Value-added tax, or VAT (BTW in the Netherlands) is 6% to 19%, depending on the amount and product you are purchasing, but non-E.U. visitors can get a refund if they spend 182€ or more in any store that participates in the VAT refund program. The shops will give you a form, which you must get stamped at Customs (allow extra time). Customs may ask to see your purchase, so don't pack it in your checked luggage. Mark the paperwork to request a credit card refund, otherwise you'll be stuck with a check in euros. Another option is to ask for a **GLOBAL REFUND FORM** (☎ 800/566-9828; www.globalrefund.com) when you make your purchase, and take it to a Global Refund counter at the airport. Your money is refunded on the spot, minus a commission.

TELEPHONES Public phones are found in cafes, post offices, and occasionally on the street. Coin-operated telephones are rare. Most phones take prepaid calling cards, which are available at kiosks, post offices, and currency-exchange stands. They cost 5€ or 10€. To make a **DIRECT INTERNATIONAL CALL,** first dial 00, then dial the country code, the area code, and the local number. The country code for the **U.S. AND CANADA** is 1; **GREAT**

BRITAIN, 44; **IRELAND,** 353; **AUSTRALIA,** 61; and **NEW ZEALAND,** 64. You can also call the U.S., Canada, the U.K., Ireland, Australia, or New Zealand using **USA DIRECT/AT&T WORLD CONNECT,** which allows you to avoid hotel surcharges. Call ☎ 0800/022-9111.

For operator assistance, call ☎ 0800/0410.

TICKETS   The best outlet is the very centrally located Uit Buro (AUB) Ticketshop, Leidseplein 26 (☎ 0900/0191; www.uitburo.nl). You can buy tickets on their website prior to your arrival. You can also ask your concierge to book tickets for you at the time that you book your room.

TIPPING   In cafes and restaurants, waiter service is usually included, though you can round the bill up or leave some small change if you like. A service charge is included in taxi fares, but a small tip (1€) is always appreciated. If you make the driver wait or are going on a long expensive trip, tip 5%. Tip hotel porters 1€ to 1.50€ for each piece of luggage.

TOILETS   If you use a toilet at a brown cafe or restaurant, it's customary to make some small purchase.

TOURIST OFFICES   For tourist information, the best outlets are the official offices of VVV Amsterdam, platform 2 inside Centraal Station, ☎ 0900/400-4040) or at Leidseplein 1 on the corner of Leidsestraat.

TOURS   The two largest tour companies are **GLOBUS/COSMOS** (☎ 800/338-7092; www.globusandcosmos.com) and **TRAFALGAR** (☎ 800/854-0103; www.trafalgartours.com). Many major airlines offer air/land package deals that include tours of Amsterdam; ask the airlines or your travel agent for details.

TRAVELERS WITH DISABILITIES
Nearly all modern hotels in Amsterdam now have rooms designed for people with disabilities, but many older hotels do not. The Netherlands Board of Tourism publishes a *Holland for the Handicapped* brochure that you can pick up at any VVV office. Not all trams in Amsterdam are fully accessible for wheelchairs, but the new trams being introduced on some routes have low central doors that are accessible. Amsterdam's Metro system is fully accessible.

Amsterdam: **A Brief History**

1200 Fishermen establish a coastal settlement at the mouth of the Amstel River, which is dammed to control periodic flooding; the settlement takes the name "Aemstelledamme."

1300 The Bishop of Utrecht grants Amsterdam its first town charter.

1323 Amsterdam's economy receives a boost when it is declared a toll center for beer.

1350 Amsterdam becomes a transit point for imported grain, which

gives it further importance as a trade center.

1602 Foundation of the United East India Company (V.O.C.), destined to become a powerful force in Holland's golden age of discovery, exploration, and trade.

1611 First Amsterdam Stock Exchange opens.

1613 Construction begins on the Herengracht, Keizersgracht, and Prinsengracht canals.

1631 Rembrandt, at age 25, moves to Amsterdam from his native Leiden.

1795 Velvet Revolution. French troops occupy Holland with the aid of Dutch revolutionaries and establish the Batavian Republic; William V flees to England.

1806–10 Louis Bonaparte, Napoleon's brother, reigns as king of Holland.

1813 The Netherlands regains independence from the French.

1910 A flushable water system for the canals is introduced.

1920 Dutch airline KLM launches the world's first scheduled air service, between Amsterdam and London.

1928 Amsterdam Olympics.

1932 Afsluitdijk (Enclosure Dike) at the head of the Zuiderzee is completed, transforming the sea on which Amsterdam stands into the freshwater IJsselmeer lake.

1940 On May 10 Nazi Germany invades the Netherlands, which surrenders 4 days later.

1944–45 Thousands die during the "Hunger Winter," when Nazi occupation forces blockade of western Holland.

1945 On May 5 German forces in the Netherlands surrender.

1960S The city takes on the mantle of Europe's hippie capital.

1975 Amsterdam's 700th anniversary. Cannabis use is decriminalized.

1987 The *Homomonument,* the world's first public memorial to persecuted gays and lesbians, is unveiled.

2001 The world's first same-sex marriage with a legal status identical to heterosexual matrimony takes place in Amsterdam.

2002 Euro banknotes and coins replace the guilder. Crown Prince Willem Alexander marries Argentine Máxima Zorreguieta in the city's Nieuwe Kerk.

2004 The former Queen Juliana dies. Controversial film director Theo van Gogh, 47, is stabbed and shot to death on the streets of Amsterdam.

Golden Age Art

Although there were earlier Dutch artists, Dutch art came into its own during the 17th-century Golden Age. Artists were blessed with wealthy patrons whose support allowed them to give free rein to their talents. The primary art patrons were Protestant merchants who commissioned portraits, genre scenes, and still lifes, not the kind of religious works commissioned by the Church in Catholic countries. The Dutch were particularly fond of pictures that depicted their world: landscapes, seascapes, domestic scenes, and portraits.

Gerrit van Honthorst

The roots of 17th-century Dutch realism are found in the work of Belgian **Jan van Eyck** (1395–1441). Early 17th-century Utrecht artist **Gerrit van Honthorst** (1590–1656), who had studied in Rome with Caravaggio, brought the new "realism of light and dark," or chiaroscuro, technique to Holland, where he influenced Dutch artists like the young Rembrandt. Best known for lively company scenes such as *The Supper Party* (ca. 1620; Uffizi, Florence), which depicted ordinary people against a plain background and set a style that continued in Dutch art for many years, Honthorst often used multiple hidden light sources to heighten the dramatic contrast of lights and darks.

Jacob van Ruisdael

Among the great landscape artists of this period, **Jacob van Ruisdael** (1628–82) stands out. In his paintings, human figures either do not appear at all or are shown as almost insignificantly small; vast skies filled with moody clouds often cover two-thirds of the canvas. His *Windmill at Wijk bij Duurstede* (ca.1665), which you can view in the city's Rijksmuseum, combines many characteristic elements of his style: The windmill stands in a somber landscape, containing a few small human figures, with a cloud-laden sky and a foreground of agitated water and reeds.

Frans Hals

Frans Hals (ca.1580–1666), the undisputed leader of the Haarlem school (schools differed from city to city), was a great portrait painter whose relaxed, informal, and naturalistic portraits contrast strikingly with the traditional formal masks of Renaissance portraits. His light brushstrokes help convey immediacy and intimacy, making his works perceptive psychological portraits. He had a genius for comic characters, showing men and women as they are and a little less than they are, as in *Malle Babbe* (1650). As a stage designer of group portraits, Hals's skill is almost unmatched—only Rembrandt is superior. Although he carefully arranged and posed each group, balancing the directions of gesture and glance, his *alla prima* brushwork (direct laying down of pigment) makes these public images—such as *The Archers of St. Aidan* (1633)—seem spontaneous. It's

worth taking a day trip to Haarlem just to visit the Frans Halsmuseum and view such works as his *A Banquet of the Officers of the St. George Militia* (ca.1627).

Rembrandt

The great genius of the period was **Rembrandt Harmenszoon van Rijn** (1606–69), one of few artists of any period to be known simply by his first name. This painter, whose works hang in places of honor in the world's great museums, may be *the* most famous Amsterdammer, both to outsiders and today's city residents.

Rembrandt pushed the art of chiaroscuro to unprecedented heights. In his paintings the values of light and dark gradually and softly blend together; this may have diffused some of the drama of chiaroscuro, but it achieved a more truthful appearance. Rembrandt's art seemed capable of revealing the soul and inner life of his subjects, and to view his series of 60 self-portraits is to see a remarkable documentation of his own psychological and physical evolution. The *Self-Portrait with Saskia*, in the Museum Het Rembrandthuis, shows him with his wife at a prosperous time when he was being commissioned to do portraits of many wealthy merchants. Later self-portraits are more psychologically complex, often depicting a careworn old man whose gaze is nonetheless sharp, compassionate, and wise.

In group portraits like *The Night Watch* (1642) and *The Syndics of the Cloth Guild* (1662), both in the Rijksmuseum, each individual portrait is done with care. The unrivaled harmony of light, color, and movement of these works is a marvel to be appreciated. Compare, too, these robust, masculine works with the tender *The Jewish Bride* (ca. 1665), also in the Rijksmuseum.

In later years Rembrandt was at the height of his artistic powers, but his contemporaries judged his work to be too personal and eccentric. Some considered him a tasteless painter who was obsessed with the ugly and ignorant of color; this opinion prevailed until the 19th century, when Rembrandt's genius was reevaluated.

Vermeer

Jan Vermeer (1632–75) of Delft is perhaps the best known of the "little Dutch masters" who specialized in one genre of painting, such as portraiture. Although they confined their artistry within a narrow scope, these painters rendered their subjects with an exquisite care and faithfulness to their actual appearances.

Vermeer's work centers on the simple pleasures and activities of domestic life—a woman pouring milk or reading a letter, for example—and all of his simple figures positively glow with color and light. Vermeer placed the figure (usually just one, but sometimes two or more) at the center of his paintings against a background in which furnishings often provided the horizontal and vertical balance, giving the composition a feeling of stability and serenity. Art historians have determined that Vermeer used mirrors and the camera obscura, an early camera, as compositional aids. A master at lighting interior scenes and rendering true colors, Vermeer was able to create an illusion of three-dimensionality in works such as *The Love Letter* (ca. 1670), in Amsterdam's Rijksmuseum. As light—usually afternoon sunshine pouring in from an open window—moves across the picture plane, it caresses and modifies all the colors.

Jan Steen

Jan Steen (ca. 1626–79), born in Leiden, painted marvelous interior scenes, often satirical and didactic in their intent. The allusions on which much of the satire depends may escape most of us today, but any viewer can appreciate the fine drawing, subtle color shading, and warm light that pervades such paintings as *Woman at Her Toilet* and *The Feast of St. Nicholas,* both in the Rijksmuseum. Many of his pictures revel in bawdy tavern scenes fueled by overindulgence in beer and gin.

Useful Phrases & Menu Terms

Useful Words & Phrases

ENGLISH	DUTCH	PRONUNCIATION
Hello	Dag/Hallo	*dakh/ha-loh*
Good morning	Goedenmorgen	*khoo-yuh-mor-khun*
Good afternoon/evening	Goedenavond	*khoo-yuhn-af-ond*
How are you?	Hoe gaat het met U?	*hoo khaht et met oo?*
Very well	Uitstekend	*out-stayk-end*
Thank you	Dank U wel	*dahnk oo wel*
Good-bye	Dag/Tot Ziens	*dakh/tot zeenss*
Good night	Goedenacht	*khoo-duh-nakht*
See you later	Tot straks	*Tot strahkss*

ENGLISH	DUTCH	PRONUNCIATION
Please	Alstublieft	*ahl-stoo-bleeft*
Yes	Ja	*yah*
No	Neen	*nay*
Excuse me	Pardon	*par-dawn*
Sorry	Sorry	*so-ree*
Do you speak English?	Spreekt U Engels?	*spraykt oo eng-els*
Can you help me?	Kunt U mij helpen?	*koont oo may-ee hel-pen?*
Give me . . .	Geeft U mij . . .	*khayft oo may . . .*
Where is . . . ?	Waar is . . . ?	*vahr iz . . . ?*
the station	het station	*het stah-ssyonh*
the post office	het postkantoor	*het post-kan-tohr*
a bank	een bank	*ayn bank*
a hotel	een hotel	*ayn ho-tel*
a restaurant	een restaurant	*ayn res-to-rahng*
a pharmacy/chemist	een apotheek	*ayn a-po-tayk*
the toilet	het toilet	*het twah-let*
To the right	Rechts	*rekhts*
To the left	Links	*links*
Straight ahead	Rechtdoor	*rekht-doar*
I would like . . .	Ik zou graag . . .	*ik zow khrakh . . .*
to eat	eten	*ay-ten*
a room for one night	een kamer voor een nacht	*ayn kah-mer voor ayn nakht*
How much is it?	Hoe veel kost het?	*hoo fayl kawst het*
The check	De rekening	*duh ray-ken-ing*
When?	Wanneer?	*vah-neer*
Yesterday	Gisteren	*khis-ter-en*
Today	Vandaag	*van-dahkh*
Tomorrow	Morgen	*mor-khen*
Breakfast	Ontbijt	*ohnt-bayt*
Lunch	Lunch	*lunch*
Dinner	Diner	*dee-nay*

Numbers

ENGLISH	DUTCH	PRONUNCIATION
one	een	*ayn*
two	twee	*tway*
three	drie	*dree*
four	vier	*veer*
five	vijf	*vayf*
six	zes	*zes*
seven	zeven	*zay-vun*
eight	acht	*akht*
nine	negen	*nay-khen*
ten	tien	*teen*
eleven	elf	*elf*
twelve	twaalf	*tvahlf*
thirteen	dertien	*dayr-teen*
fourteen	veertien	*vayr-teen*
fifteen	vijftien	*vayf-teen*

ENGLISH	DUTCH	PRONUNCIATION
sixteen	zestien	*zes-teen*
seventeen	zeventien	*zay-vun-teen*
eighteen	achtien	*akh-teen*
nineteen	negentien	*nay-khun-teen*
twenty	twintig	*twin-tikh*

Days of the Week

ENGLISH	DUTCH	PRONUNCIATION
Monday	Maandag	*mahn-dakh*
Tuesday	Dinsdag	*deens-dakh*
Wednesday	Woensdag	*voohns-dakh*
Thursday	Donderdag	*donder-dakh*
Friday	Vrijdag	*vray-dakh*
Saturday	Zaterdag	*zahter-dakh*
Sunday	Zondag	*zohn-dakh*

Months

ENGLISH	DUTCH	PRONUNCIATION
January	Januari	*yahn-oo-aree*
February	Februari	*fayhb-roo-aree*
March	Maart	*mahrt*
April	April	*ah-pril*
May	Mai	*mah-eey*
June	Juni	*yoo-nee*
July	Juli	*yoo-lee*
August	August	*awh-khoost*
September	September	*sep-tem-buhr*
October	Oktober	*oct-oah-buhr*
November	November	*noa-vem-buhr*
December	December	*day-sem-buhr*

Dutch Menu Savvy

BASICS	
ontbijt	breakfast
lunch	lunch
diner	dinner
boter	butter
boterham	sandwich
brood	bread
stokbrood	French bread
voorgerechten	starters
honing	honey
hoofdgerechten	main courses
hutspot	mashed potatoes and carrots
jam	jam
kaas	cheese
mosterd	mustard
pannekoeken	pancakes
peper	pepper
saus	sauce
suiker	sugar

SOUPS (SOEPEN)

zout	salt
aardappelsoep	potato soup
bonensoep	bean soup
erwtensoep	pea soup (usually includes bacon or sausage)
groentensoep	vegetable soup
kippensoep	chicken soup
soep	soup
tomatensoep	tomato soup
uiensoep	onion soup

EGGS (EIER)

eieren	eggs
hardgekookte eieren	hard-boiled eggs
omelette	omelet
roereieren	scrambled eggs
spiegeleieren	fried eggs
uitsmijter	fried eggs and ham on bread
zachtgekookte eieren	boiled eggs

FISH (VIS)

forel	trout
garnalen	prawns
gerookte zalm	smoked salmon
haring	herring
kabeljauw	cod
kreeft	lobster
makreel	mackerel
mosselen	mussels
oesters	oysters
paling	eel
sardienen	sardines
schelvis	haddock
schol	plaice
tong	sole
zalm	salmon

MEATS (VLEES)

bief	beef
biefstuk	steak
eend	duck
tricandeau	roast pork
gans	goose
gehakt	minced meat
haasbiefstuk	filet steak
ham	ham
kalfsvlees	veal
kalkoen	turkey
kip	chicken
konijn	rabbit
koude schotel	cold cuts
lamscotelet	lamb chops

lamsvlees	lamb
lever	liver
ragout	beef stew
rookvlees	smoked meat
runder	beef
spek	bacon
worst	sausage

VEGETABLES & SALADS *(GROENTEN/SLA)*

aardappelen	potatoes
asperges	asparagus
augurken	pickles
bieten	beets
bloemkool	cauliflower
bonen	beans
champignons	mushrooms
erwten	peas
groenten	vegetables
knoflook	garlic
komkommer	cucumber
komkommersla	cucumber salad
kool	cabbage
patates frites	french fries
prei	leek
prinsesseboonen	green beans
purée	mashed potatoes
radijsen	radishes
rapen	turnips
rijst	rice
sla	lettuce, salad
spinazie	spinach
tomaten	tomatoes
uien	onions
wortelen	carrots
zuurkool	sauerkraut

DESSERTS *(NAGERECHTEN)*

appelgebak	apple pie
appelmoes	applesauce
cake	cake
compòte	stewed fruits
gebak	pastry
ijs	ice cream
jonge kaas	young cheese (mild)
koekjes	cookies
oliebollen	doughnuts
oude kaas	old cheese (strong)
room	cream
slagroom	whipped cream
smeerkaas	cheese spread
speculaas	spiced cookies

FRUITS *(VRUCHTEN)*

aapel	apple
aardbei	strawberry
ananas	pineapple
citroen	lemon
druiven	grapes
framboos	raspberry
kersen	cherries
peer	pear
perzik	peach
pruimen	plums

BEVERAGES *(DRANKEN)*

bier (or pils)	beer
cognac	brandy
fles	bottle
glas	glass
jenever	gin
koffie	coffee
melk	milk
rode wijn	red wine
thee	tea
water	water
mineraal water	sparkling water
witte wijn	white wine

COOKING TERMS

gebakken	fried
gebraden	roast
gegrild	grilled
gekookt	boiled/cooked
gerookt	smoked
geroosteerd	boiled
gestoofd	stewed
half doorbakken	rare
goed doorbakken	well done
koud	cold
niet doorbakken	rare
warm	hot

Toll-Free Numbers & Websites

AER LINGUS
☎ *800/474-7424 in the U.S.*
☎ *01/886-8844 in Ireland*
www.aerlingus.com

AIR CANADA
☎ 888/247-2262
www.aircanada.com

AIR FRANCE
☎ *800/237-2747 in the U.S.*
☎ *0820-820-820 in France*
www.airfrance.com

AIR NEW ZEALAND
☎ *800/262-1234, -2468 in the U.S.*
☎ *800/663-5494 in Canada*

☎ 0800/737-000 in New Zealand
www.airnewzealand.com

ALITALIA
☎ 800/223-5730 in the U.S.
☎ 8488-65641 in Italy
www.alitalia.it

AMERICAN AIRLINES
☎ 800/433-7300
www.aa.com

AUSTRIAN AIRLINES
☎ 800/843-0002 in the U.S.
☎ 43/(0)5-1789 in Austria
www.aua.com

BMI
No U.S. number
☎ 0870/6070-222 in Britain
www.flybmi.com

BRITISH AIRWAYS
☎ 800/247-9297 in the U.S.
☎ 0870/850-9-850 in Britain
www.british-airways.com

CONTINENTAL AIRLINES
☎ 800/525-0280
www.continental.com

DELTA AIR LINES
☎ 800/221-1212
www.delta.com

EASYJET
No U.S. number
☎ 0905 821 0905 in the U.K.
www.easyjet.com

IBERIA
☎ 800/772-4642 in the U.S.
☎ 902/400-500 in Spain
www.iberia.com

ICELANDAIR
☎ 800/223-5500 in the U.S.
☎ 354/50-50-100 in Iceland
www.icelandair.is

KLM
☎ 800/374-7747 in the U.S.
☎ 020/4-747-747 in the Netherlands
www.klm.nl

LUFTHANSA
☎ 800/645-3880 in the U.S.
☎ 180-5-838426 in Germany
www.lufthansa.com

NORTHWEST AIRLINES
☎ 800/225-2525
www.nwa.com

QANTAS
☎ 800/227-4500 in the U.S.
☎ 612/131313 in Australia
www.qantas.com

SCANDINAVIAN AIRLINES
☎ 800/221-2350 in the U.S.
☎ 0070/727-727 in Sweden
☎ 70/10-20-00 in Denmark
☎ 358/(0)20-386-000 in Finland
☎ 815/200-400 in Norway
www.scandinavian.net

SOUTH AFRICAN AIRLINES
☎ 800/722-9675 in the U.S.
☎ 0861/359-722 in South Africa
www.flysaa.com

SWISS INTERNATIONAL AIRLINES
☎ 877/359-7947 in the U.S.
☎ 0848/85-2000 in Switzerland
www.swiss.com

UNITED AIRLINES
☎ 800/241-6522
www.united.com

US AIRWAYS
☎ 800/428-4322
www.usairways.com

VIRGIN ATLANTIC AIRWAYS
☎ 800/862-8621 in continental U.S.
☎ 0870/380-2007 in Britain
www.virgin-atlantic.com

Photo **Credits**